STORIES
FROM THE
SIDELINES

Malinda Fugate's excellent examination of those who are supporting players, not the super stars, is fascinating reading. *Stories from the Sidelines* reveals accounts of lesser-known people in the Bible as well as provides alternate perspectives to familiar narratives. Each chapter begins with a detailed retelling of Scripture, including available historical context and employing prayerful imagination to bring it to life. Highly recommended.

—Eva Shaw, Ph.D., Author

The Seer, The Finder and The Pursuer

Through these imaginatively rendered stories, Malinda invites us to believe that even when we feel sidelined, God sees us and has a purpose for our lives. Step onto the dusty roads walked by these oft-forgotten Bible characters and be reminded that God also walks with you. There is much wisdom in these pages.

—Sarah L. Sanderson, Author

The Place We Make

If you've ever wondered about your place in God's plan or heard stories of heroic faith and felt like you could never measure up, this book is for you. Malinda Fugate will take you on an eye-opening tour of the "sidelines" in Scripture, highlighting stories of overlooked characters in a way that will shift your whole perspective. You'll learn why sometimes the sidelines are exactly where we belong and why that's something to celebrate.

—Gina Dalfonzo, Author

Dorothy and Jack: The Transforming Friendship of Dorothy L. Sayers and C. S. Lewis

STORIES
FROM THE
SIDELINES

MALINDA FUGATE

AMBASSADOR INTERNATIONAL
GREENVILLE, SOUTH CAROLINA & BELFAST, NORTHERN IRELAND
www.ambassador-international.com

Stories from the Sidelines

ISBN: 978-1-64960-511-5, paperback
eISBN: 978-1-64960-554-2

Cover Design by Hannah Linder Designs
Interior Typesetting by Dentelle Design
Edited by Valerie Coffman

Scripture taken from the Holy Bible, New International Version®, NIV® Copyright ©1973, 1978, 1984, 2011 by Biblica, Inc.® Used by permission. All rights reserved worldwide.

Ambassador International titles may be purchased in bulk for education, business, fundraising, or sales promotional use. For information, please email sales@emeraldhouse.com.

AMBASSADOR INTERNATIONAL
Emerald House
411 University Ridge, Suite B14
Greenville, SC 29601
United States
www.ambassador-international.com

AMBASSADOR BOOKS
The Mount
2 Woodstock Link
Belfast, BT6 8DD
Northern Ireland, United Kingdom
www.ambassadormedia.co.uk

The colophon is a trademark of Ambassador, a Christian publishing company.

Acknowledgments

My gratitude overflows for the generous support and endless encouragement that surrounded this project. Ultimately, I thank the Lord for inspiration, direction, and for helping me overcome challenges during the process of telling sidelines stories. My incredible community of family, friends, and church would fill another book if I listed each name; but I couldn't have completed a book without your love and prayers.

Becca, Gabe, and Claudia were instrumental in making this happen by providing a peaceful retreat in the woods that inspired writing momentum.

Without JJ's continual help with the stuff that fills life and slows creative progress, I'd likely still be contemplating chapter one.

Angie, Lisa, and Sue were essential to every word and deserve a trophy for wading through such rough drafts.

Consulting with Jenny, Charyse, Brooke, and Kate solidified ideas into paragraphs, while productivity parties with Jenna, Mary Ann, and Steph kept the motivation flowing.

Cynthia and Brooke ran with me toward the finish line of releasing this book into the wild.

Finally, many thanks to the team at Ambassador International for believing in the potential of the sidelines and working to share God's story.

Table of Contents

INTRODUCTION
The View from the Sidelines

Everyone loves a hero. We cheer for people who take charge, lead the way, and save the day—and we want to be like them. They're in the spotlight, front and center, seen by all. In real life, protagonists are easy to identify with stories and circumstances that get our attention. Perhaps it's the things they do, or maybe it's their personalities. Heroes can include parents, bosses, community leaders, pastors, politicians, celebrities, athletes, even children. Sometimes, we find ourselves in that spotlight, and it feels pretty good. With accompanying encouragement from those around us, we have a sense of importance along with a feeling of significance and purpose. Who we are and what we do truly matters.

But there are other occasions where we seem to live in the shadows as the spotlight shines on someone else. We might find ourselves there frequently, feeling insignificant and unimportant. While everyone else is in the game, we're merely watching from the sidelines. From there, it's easy to believe that we're less worthy than the star player, unneeded, and ineffective. We doubt our purpose and no longer believe we have a place to belong. On the sidelines, we might be overlooked. We question if anyone cares about the sidekick when all eyes are on the hero.

Our tendency to illuminate heroes and fail to notice any others also surfaces as we study God's Word. From childhood Sunday school, we highlight the narratives of Moses and David, Peter and Paul, or Esther and Ruth. We look for their redeeming qualities while downplaying their flaws, and they become examples of who we aspire to be. As we focus on their stories, placing ordinary humans on pedestals of greatness, we shine an exclusive spotlight on their lives. Meanwhile, the people around them fade into the shadows as supporting characters. It becomes easy to forget what they did or even their names. In fact, many details aren't recorded at all, forever lost in history. Sidelines folks slip from our memory after a brief, passing glance as we breeze through the celebrated stories in Scripture.

We often celebrate the champions and ignore the ordinary in modern life, too. When this happens, we fail to notice some great treasures. We neglect precious people and overlook significant parts of a story. But there are rich lessons to learn, vital history to remember, and the beautiful presence of God to experience. We miss it in others; and tragically, we miss it in ourselves. When we're resigned to living life on the sidelines, we mistakenly assume that nothing important is happening to us or that we have little to contribute to the story. We believe we're not even worth remembering. If others don't see us and we don't value our place in the big picture, we wonder how God could possibly have any regard for us sideline-dwellers.

The truth is worthy of rejoicing! Not only does God see us in the shadows, He is with us. He designed a purpose for each moment, and the sidelines are not accidental. No, this is certainly not a case of being forgotten or discarded. We were intentionally placed in the perfect place to experience His love and take part in His plans. God's glory is often found on the sidelines, displayed in His beloved children. The hard part is looking up from our point of view and seeing His wondrous perspective.

Identifying hope when we're not the main character can be a daunting challenge, but we get to practice as we immerse ourselves in the pages of the Word. When we slow down and look around, people often labeled as minor characters reveal more dimension in frequently-told stories. Spending time in Scripture and connecting similar themes inspire us to seek our own place in God's big plan. Becoming familiar with those on the Biblical sidelines gives us the ability to see what's happening to us today, and the lens by which we view our neighbors becomes a little clearer as we see each of us through God's eyes. Once we understand that our place on the sidelines is no longer insignificant or unimportant, we realize that the Light of the World is not a spotlight; but instead, we are all illuminated in His love.

It's time to begin a quest through the back roads of familiar stories. Together, let's discover what the people on the sidelines have to say and thoughtfully consider where we fit in the narrative. We'll use available research and historical context to better understand what we read in the pages of Scripture. When information is limited, we'll utilize prayerful imagination so that we can see ancient people more completely. Hand in hand, let's walk alongside folks like Noah's sons, Gehazi, Huldah, Matthias, and Lydia. As we consider their journeys, we'll discover that Scripture contains an abundance of guidance and encouragement for our own stories. You're invited to see that we all have a place in God's kingdom, our uniqueness has purpose, and our value is not determined by human standards. We'll set aside our notions of heroes on pedestals and celebrate the gifts of the ordinary. It might change the way we see things for good.

CHAPTER 1
Shem, Ham, and Japheth

Based on Genesis 5-10

Every father has a project, but theirs had a serious undertaking. A massive structure towered above them, taking on a more distinct form with each passing year. It was understood that the three sons, Shem, Ham, and Japheth, would also devote their sweat and muscles to help their father, Noah, with what seemed to be never-ending construction. At first, they were eager to assist by carrying wood and handing him tools; and soon, they learned the craftsmanship needed to follow the Divine instructions. With pride, they looked up to Noah as a master builder; but they couldn't help but hear the way the community talked about their beloved father.

People ridiculed the desert-bound sailing vessel, mocking Noah's inexperience and declaring it a colossal waste of time and resources. But what did they expect? They thought that because Noah was different from everyone else, it was unsurprising that he would have a strange hobby. After all, the guy claimed to talk to God and kept his family separate from the rest of their neighbors. They assumed that he thought he was superior to all of them, and no one was interested in being insulted by an amateur carpenter.

To Shem, Ham, and Japheth, the boat was simply a fact of life. They inherited their father's work ethic, along with his faith in God, despite the occasional doubts that a promised flood would ever carry this ark above rising currents. It was better to have safety than regrets, and Noah's approach to life was kinder and gentler than the rough ways of the surrounding people. A few acquaintances were friendly, though time would prove that their values and morality mirrored that of the general population. Remarkably, each of the sons met women willing to leave their selfish ways and follow the God of Noah and his family. Now they were a family of eight serving the Lord together in the most unconventional way. Their lives reflected the goodness of God, but all everyone else seemed to see was a giant boat on dry ground.

The ark was nearly complete, and the men understood the grave situation. Everything they knew would be destroyed by the flood, leaving them to care for the surviving animals and begin life again. Their trust in God's plan was steadfast, but the responsibility weighed heavily on their shoulders. Attempts to warn their neighbors fell on unbelieving ears and merely resulted in more scorn heaped upon the family. With heavy hearts, Shem, Ham, and Japheth obediently worked, waiting to learn what their father heard from the Lord. The final boards were fitted into place; pitch was applied to make the vessel watertight; and an abundance of food was stockpiled onboard. The final days had come.

"It's time," came the soft but resolute words from Noah. Together, they gathered their possessions and made their way to the ship that had been the focus of all their days. Just as they were about to step through the gaping door of the ark, Japheth's wife exclaimed, "Look!"

Any doubts that may have lingered were erased at the sight before them. A menagerie of every animal they could imagine, as well as some they had never dreamed existed, made its way toward them. In seven pairs each, the creatures arrived to board the ark as if they were gathering at the local watering hole. Though the more timid species gave the predators plenty of space, there were surprisingly no scuffles or threats. The next seven days were spent arranging their newly assembled zoo among the three massive decks, making everyone comfortable as clouds gathered in the sky above them.

Finally, their feet left the familiar ground one last time as they joined their animal charges aboard the boat. An abrupt crash resounded through the vessel, causing the floor to shake under their feet. The Lord had shut the door just as the sound of raindrops could be heard on the rooftop. The following moments would be etched into their memories for the rest of their lives.

Sprinkles grew into a pounding rain as the sky burst open and water fell over the entire land. Springs exploded from the ground, quickly creating pools in the low-lying valleys that began to rise. The family marveled at the wondrous work of the Lord while their community stared in disbelief. The people never thought there was any substance to old Noah's claims of a flood in their dry climate. Yet, here they stood, soaking wet and wading in newly formed streams. The shock quickly transformed into panic as the water crept past their knees. Everyone scrambled for higher ground, but options were limited. Babies shrieked while their fathers tried to hold them above the fast-moving currents. Mothers screamed as their children fought to keep their heads above water, and they were soon lost to the rushing deluge. There was only one hope—Noah's boat!

Shem, Ham, and Japheth closed their eyes, wishing their ears weren't hearing the slaps of hands against the wooden hull and desperate pleas for help. Angry shouts intensified and mixed with the gurgle of rising flood waters, but the door could no longer be safely opened. Their accusations, apologies, and grasps at life were dampened by the storm and the thick walls of the boat. Cries became weaker and the rain stronger, until the entire ark abruptly began to rock back and forth, floating atop the current. Soon, all they could hear was the steady pounding of water above them and the symphony of animal noises around them. The tears of the surviving family silently fell, mourning the life and the community they once knew, now lost forever.

A month never seemed so long, but they counted forty rainy days before a hush fell over the ark. The steady drumming of rain ceased, leaving a strange lull. The waves lapped against the side of the ship as the animal's occasional murmurs echoed off the ship's walls. After a moment's pause, the family continued the never-ending task of caring for the creatures in their charge—a sweaty, smelly, difficult job. They watched their step in the corners, not wanting to disturb a snake hidden in the hay. Japheth always gave a little extra attention to the horses, while Ham's wife snuck an extra snack to the elephants, fascinated by their long trunks. They tried to comfort one another as they grieved the loss of people they knew and the land they had lived upon, but their true Source of strength was the Lord.

Noah reminded them that God's ways, though often difficult to comprehend, were beyond the ways of humans and always perfect. They prayed and worshiped, not knowing when they would leave the boat or what to expect from life after the flood. The family trusted God in this strange new routine, though the ark felt more confining as time stretched on. They only had each other, these creatures, and water—lots and lots of water.

One hundred fifty days had passed when the wind began to blow. The sound whistled through the upper deck of the ark, its mournful song waking the family from sleep. Soon, it, too, became part of their routine, bringing a lingering sense of hope. Something was different. One afternoon, a sudden jolt shook the ark once more, and then, stillness. The family nearly fell over as their legs, so accustomed to the rolling of the sea, found the floor beneath them firm and steady. They no longer heard the rhythm of waves hitting the hull. Only quiet graced their ears as they looked at one another in wonder. No one said a word, but they knew they had landed. A glance out the window revealed that they were perched atop a mountain, with a sea still spread out around them. The wait continued.

More than another month later, Noah called his sons up to the window. Together, they released a raven, watching it expectantly as it spread its wings and soared over the watery expanse. But its return told them it wasn't yet safe for them to venture off the boat. Sometime later, they sent a dove out as a scout, and it, too, returned. A week later, the dove had a second chance to be their lookout and rewarded them with a treasure—a leaf from an olive tree.

That night, Shem, Ham, and Japheth discussed what would happen next in their new life. They didn't know what to expect, but the prospect of setting foot onto firm ground, breathing in fresh clean air, and feeling the wide open space around them sounded like paradise.

Another week passed, and the men released the dove again. They watched and waited until she flew out of sight, keeping their eyes on the horizon for her return. What earthly delight might she bring this time? The afternoon stretched on into evening, and the light began to seep from the sky, yet the dove did not come back. One by one, stars emerged from the darkness; and Noah knew the bird had found freedom. Now, the faithful family could find their freedom, too.

"The Lord has spoken; it's time to depart!" Noah exclaimed to his wife, sons, and daughters-in-law. They opened the massive door, and the animals made their way into the bright sunlight. Noah, Shem, Ham, Japheth, and the women tenderly stepped from their life-saving ark onto the newly-dried ground beneath them. The family watched as the creatures they had spent months tending scattered over the landscape, each going their own way.

When the last hoof step had faded, it was time to worship God; so the sons helped their father construct an altar to sacrifice burnt offerings. The Lord gave them His promise to never curse the ground again because of humans, despite any evilness in their hearts. Never again would He destroy living creatures in this way. As long as the earth remains, seasons would continue; and day and night would maintain their steady rhythm. The family was instructed to be fruitful and repopulate the land; and as they heard the words of God, they marveled at a beautiful array of color spread across the clouds. Rainbows would appear again, reminding them of God's covenant. Shem, Ham, and Japheth believed the Lord, not merely because of their father's instructions but through their own faith that had grown from walking in obedience.

Life settled into a new quiet routine, much welcomed after days of rain and adventure inside the ark. Noah planted a vineyard; and the family watched it take root, grow, and thrive. They enjoyed the fruit of their labor, but a day came when Noah drank too much of its wine. That afternoon, Ham wandered into Noah's tent and discovered him drunk and naked. Immediately, he ran to tell his brothers, who calmly secured a garment, held it between them, and walked backward into their father's tent. Averting their gaze away from the disgraced and vulnerable man, they gently covered him and left him to sleep off the stupor.

Once awake and sober, Noah was enraged to discover Ham's disrespect. He cursed the sons of Ham while blessing Shem and Japheth and their family line. The days and centuries were lived out according to Noah's words, and the tales of the family who survived the flood continue to fill the pages of our history.

•••••••••••••••••••••••••••••••••

Extreme circumstances united three brothers who were set apart from friends and neighbors. Selfish ambition did not direct their lives; but instead, they were led by the God of their father. Building a large ark was a massive undertaking, and the intensity of their life's work could have been magnified by opposition and mockery from the community. Forecasting mass destruction probably did not award them popularity. In fact, the average neighbor would likely have been insulted by the notion that a deity would disapprove of their lifestyle and threaten annihilation. But the weight of the community's opinion would have been feather-light compared to the heaviness that came with the consequences of disobedience to the Lord. Shem, Ham, and Japheth lived each day with the knowledge that everything and everyone would be destroyed. Confronting that reality while devoting themselves to ark-building could have strained their mental and emotional health. Did they ever struggle with doubt? Were there moments of anger when they felt the whole situation was extreme or unfair? As they processed everything that was about to happen, they remained committed to following the Lord. Noah's family served God steadfastly from the first nail they hammered to their first days on dry land. Whenever they felt alone, they knew they had the Lord and each other.

Not only did they survive incredible trauma but they also persisted in faithfulness, despite the turmoil surrounding them. No modern-day dystopian book or movie could prepare any of us for the actual reality of living through the destruction of the world. Everything wiped away, mass casualties, and uncountable loss is nothing a person could handle without the strength that comes from God. Even now, we grapple with the contrasts between God's nurture and His wrath found in the Old Testament. Noah's family lived in that tension, their human minds trying to understand the ways of Almighty God. Whatever they understood and however many questions remained, they stood firmly in their belief in the Lord.

This shared experience also united the family. They were the only ones who truly understood and could relate to one another. They knew that it was one thing to serve God when life went smoothly, but to worship Him through world destruction brought a new level of intensity to their devotion. They also likely knew the indescribable gratitude after being saved from devastation, as well as the heavy burden of survivor's guilt when they remembered their neighbors who had refused to be saved. These eight people alone knew what it was like to carry the overwhelming responsibility of building a dependable boat, keeping the animals alive, then facing the enormous task of reestablishing a new civilization. In their loneliness, their bonds as a family were likely reinforced.

Shem, Ham, and Japheth initially appear to be on the sidelines while Noah takes the starring role in this story. But their experience was as fully traumatic and inspiring as their father's. They were not just along for the carpentry apprenticeship or a rainy-day cruise; the brothers had to determine for themselves if they believed Noah's claims about God. They were faced with the choice to follow Him, too, or join their neighbors' immorality. They endured contempt, back-breaking work in the desert heat, and a crash course in animal husbandry. They made it through a storm like they'd never seen before and survived a long period of confinement at sea without knowing when they'd step back on land again. Shem, Ham, and Japheth were not merely spectators; they were fully in the game.

Being on the sidelines doesn't indicate that our experience is any less meaningful than that of others. It doesn't make us less important or unnecessary. Sometimes, when we look at a professional with an assistant, we hold the assistant in lower regard, assuming they are less capable than the professional. We often fail to acknowledge the hard work, extra hours, and excessive skills of the assistant; then we forget that the professional could not accomplish the job without help. Without his family, Noah would not have been able to complete the mission to build a massive watercraft, care for each creature, and repopulate the earth. His sons were not of any lower status, nor did they have fewer responsibilities.

When we dismiss folks on the sidelines, it also affects our self-perception when we find ourselves in a similar position. Our diminished view of the sidelines can carry over to a devalued view of our own time there. However, we will soon find that sidelines life is full of significance. Following God's plan required them all to work together.

The brothers' contribution to humanity is clearly impactful. They had a crucial role in saving the world and their obedience to God resulted in the continuation of life on earth. While we can be thankful for that alone, there are a few other truths we can take from their time on the outer edges of this story.

The first thing we examine is their example of integrity in adversity. Their faithfulness to God placed them at odds with the culture around them. Like fighting to sail against a raging current, living with a different worldview than our surrounding community is an exhausting battle. Yet Shem, Ham, and Japheth demonstrated not only that it's possible, but that it's necessary. Had they compromised on God's instructions, it would have been the difference between life and death.

It's crucial to have discernment when we are living counter-culturally. When the stakes are high, we must be certain that we're heeding the Holy Spirit and being obedient to the Lord. We have a grave responsibility to accurately understand God's Word. If Noah merely had a casual relationship with God, would he have completely understood his instructions? Declaring the destruction of all humankind was serious business and needed to be the truth. Most of all, it required the immense love of God. The dire news needed to be given with care and with a goal to rescue, calling the people to draw near to God. Had Shem, Ham, and Japheth shouted judgment from the town square, only calling out condemnation without a solution, it wouldn't have been loving nor helpful. Instead, they reported what they heard from the Lord and went about the business of following His directions. They spent more time building the ark than advertising the flood. The message was loud and clear but not vindictive. As we learn from the brothers on the sidelines, we need to keep this in mind. The world does not need more armchair couch potato judgment, and God doesn't need our help to determine what is right and wrong.

We have been given the truth in His Word and a purpose to fulfill. We can't have a surface-level relationship with God and then expect to completely comprehend His message. When we find ourselves about to step on a soapbox, we might instead take a step back. We're not the saviors of this world; we are humble disciples sojourning together, seeking God's truth and growing in faith. We must be immersed in Scripture and in His presence in order to fully comprehend His message. Seeking God's truth in a community of faith keeps us accountable and helps us understand more fully. That deep, humble comprehension is required when we are living counter-culturally, and God's truth doesn't match the beliefs of the people around us. When we remember that we are all humans trying our best to understand the Divine, it alters our approach. We become fellow seekers instead of superior judges. This involves sharing our understanding as well as listening to fellow disciples share what they have learned.

The next step is to focus on God's instructions found in His Word. When we feel that we are being led to do something, it's imperative to be sure it truly aligns with Scripture. Then, how we serve God speaks louder than any descriptive words. We can talk about love, or we can live it. But love is merely a concept if it's not put into action; and without love, we are nothing but a noisy clanging cymbal.[1]

Making noise is necessary at times. If someone is about to walk into a pit, yelling, "Look out!" might save the unsuspecting walker from injury. But covering the pit or creating a safety barrier would be even better. Filling the pit would be a long-term solution that would eliminate the problem. Actions are more effective, and God uses those motivated by love to make a difference. As we look at Shem, Ham, and Japheth, we notice that it's not their words but their behavior that fills their chapters in Genesis.

The brothers are also an example of staying the course, enduring in faith, despite obstacles. Scholars estimate that it took approximately one hundred years to build the ark. That leaves plenty of time for doubts, second-guessing, and changing of minds. A lot of arguments against the project probably surfaced in their minds during those decades of hard labor. The lack of rain in a century could persuade someone that a storm in the forecast was illogical. Any difficulties might have discouraged them. Yet Noah and his sons diligently continued and completed their task. Then they took their resolve aboard the ark and completed their mission. All of this was possible by the power of God. He sustained them and guided them through every question and obstacle.

As we look back on Ham, Shem, and Japheth's journey, we have a privilege not given to the brothers. Our bird's eye hindsight view reveals how each moment had a bigger purpose. The entire world was affected by these events then and through the ages, all the way to today's children hearing the story for the first time. Yet Noah and his family couldn't see the big picture. They

---

1   1 Corinthians 13:1

didn't know how their faithfulness would resound for generations, their legacy stretching beyond the task of preserving humanity. They were unaware that every single plank of gopher wood mattered, that even the basic acts of perseverance would affect those who learned from their example.

So it goes with us. When we stand faithfully on the sidelines, focused on the tasks before us, we can rarely see beyond our current circumstances. We don't have the luxury of knowing how far God is reaching with our humble obedience. There's no way to see future results of our actions or who might also feel their effects. Though God sometimes reveals pieces of His plan to us, we often find ourselves trusting in the unseen, taking a moment at a time, and praying that the Lord will use our offerings for His glory.

We are encouraged that nothing given lovingly from the heart of a Christ-follower is wasted. When we trust by faith while our sight is obscured, we remain steadfast, despite obstacles and challenges. Like Noah and his sons, we can continue communicating with the Lord, asking questions, listening for instruction, and relying on His peace in the quiet times when His voice isn't clear. It's not a requirement that we see everything that He has in mind before we agree to follow Him. Our obedience is not conditional on reviewing blueprints from start to finish. Moment by moment, we can follow the direction we are given while being encouraged that there is so much more happening beyond our vantage point. Our todays matter. What might appear to be a small act of faithfulness is a beautiful gift presented to the God Who loves us passionately. Our time on the sidelines is a crucial contribution to His larger plan, as essential as a plank of wood in a giant boat.

CHAPTER 2
Lot's Wife

Based on Genesis 11–14 and 19

Growing up in Sodom produced boldness. The city reveled in its freedom: a place where religion and morality were open to individual interpretation and wealth could be gained at any cost. People respected whatever it took to be successful. It was understood that each person was responsible for their own well-being, a task to be taken seriously in a land where deception and manipulation were acceptable means to getting what one desired. The strong were more successful than the weak in Sodom, and the shrewd were rewarded for their persistence.

There was a young woman who was proud to have been born in this thriving town, one of a handful of cities on the fertile green plain. Independence coursed through her veins, and she felt most alive bargaining at the marketplace. Her father always gave his daughter the best advantages, and her mother taught her the ways that a woman in Sodom could succeed. Men might be in authority, but the wives of the most powerful had great influence. Therefore, the young woman knew that whom she married was important. When a rich foreigner proposed, she was both intrigued and surprised that her father accepted the match.

The man's name was Lot; and until recently, he had been living out on the plains with his abundant livestock and servants. His interest in city life was unexpectedly welcomed by townspeople who were known for rejecting outsiders. Was his great wealth the ticket to enter freely? Clearly, he was a man of power to have so many people working for him, tending his herds while he demonstrated business skills inside Sodom's gates. Perhaps others were as curious as the woman about Lot's calm demeanor and mysterious worship of a strange God. He wasn't afraid that someone would take advantage of his kindness; and he maintained his integrity, even when dealing with Sodom's most influential leaders. Before long, his presence in the city and their marriage became as comfortable and familiar as the streets the woman had walked her whole life. Sodom was home.

The murmurs of unrest grew from rumor to reality much too quickly. War began as a distant threat that moved close to home with frightening speed. The night Sodom fell was marked by terrifying darkness. The sound of approaching soldiers grew louder as they overcame the city walls and flooded the woman's beloved streets. Screams of neighbors blended with shouts of war. Doors were thrown open, dishes shattered, and fearful protests silenced with threats of death. The enemy's men took everything the Sodomites had worked for—from food and household goods to treasures of wealth.

Lot and his wife knew they weren't safe in their home but couldn't imagine that they would find escape outside of their walls. Lot began to pray to his God for rescue, but his words were drowned out by the crash of their door breaking open as soldiers invaded their house. Before Lot's wife could cry out for help, a firm hand covered her mouth; and a muscular arm pinned her to the wall. Lot reached for his staff to fight them off, but he was quickly outnumbered and subdued by the soldiers.

Lot and his wife helplessly watched the ransacking of their precious possessions, aware that material loss was the least of their trouble. The muscular soldier, damp with sweat and smelling of weeks-old body odor, threw the woman over his shoulder in one swift motion. She caught a glimpse of two other invaders binding Lot's hands and arms; and together, they were swept into the chaotic night, uncertain if they would live or die.

Treatment was rough, but their captors seemed more interested in making them march instead of killing them immediately. Leering soldiers made threatening advances; but so far, none had touched the woman beyond a push or shove. Her wrists burned from the constant rubbing of the ropes that bound her, and her stomach grumbled in hunger. Nothing compared to her thirst, however, which was intensified by the smoke from the campfires. She hoped that Lot was still praying to his God for rescue. In the brief time they had been married, she had seen prayers answered and accepted that Lot's God was as powerful as, if not more capable than, the many other gods revered in Sodom. Perhaps He would be the one to get them out of this mess, though she didn't know what kind of devastation they would find if they returned.

Night had fallen, and the woman hoped the dark would bring quiet. However, she feared that it would instead embolden the enemy soldiers to do their worst. Despite her exhaustion, she wanted to remain alert in an effort to protect herself.

Suddenly, a new sound drifted across the camp. There were more shouts and battle cries approaching! The soldiers grabbed their weapons and ran to defend their spoils of war.

The woman found Lot nearby; and together, they huddled in fear as the violence escalated. Lot opened his eyes wide and, in an outburst, declared praise to his God.

"I know them!" he whispered urgently into her ear. "They're from the house of my uncle, Abram! God heard my prayers, and deliverance has come!"

The captives huddled together as the attack unfolded around them. Minutes became tormenting hours; and the woman closed her eyes, pressing her face into Lot's shoulder. The sights and sound of slaughter were unbearable.

Suddenly, Lot pulled her to her feet. "Come on! We've got to move!" he urged.

Together, they stumbled forward, led by a rescuer from Abram's household. Lot was right. Deliverance had come.

Years later, their brief captivity faded into an occasional recurring nightmare. Their home, possessions, family, and servants had been restored, though peace of mind took longer to rebuild than repairing the damage to Sodom's streets and houses. Two beautiful daughters brought joy into the traumatized home. As the girls grew, the family made happy memories that crowded out any thoughts of the invasion.

Lot continued to excel in the public square. It seemed that people had forgotten that he wasn't a born-and-raised Sodomite, despite his quirks and devotion to a strange God. He had learned the ways of their people and fit in with the culture well enough. Their daughters, now grown, were engaged to be married to promising young men. The woman was proud of the life she had built in the city she loved. Soon, they would host a wedding, an opportunity for their success to shine among their neighbors.

One evening, Lot returned home from Sodom's gate with a bizarre surprise. He was accompanied by two guests, strangers unlike anyone the woman had ever seen. His kindness to outsiders was something that the woman never quite understood, but she attributed it to Lot's past as a foreigner himself. While he prepared something for the guests to eat, the woman made sure there was a place for them to sleep that night. She had many questions about who these men were, their origin, and their intentions.

As she was about to inquire, the stillness of evening was interrupted by footsteps at the door and a forceful knock. Deep voices could be heard outside surrounding the house. She recognized a few neighbors and men who did business with Lot. It became apparent that the crowd was growing as the noise increased.

"Where are your visitors? Introduce us! We want to . . . uh . . . get to know them!" they taunted with an edge and sinister intention that made the woman uncomfortable.

Lot made his way to the door.

"What are you doing?" the woman asked, as fear of the crowd welled up in her chest. Surely, he wouldn't let them in!

Lot slipped out the door, closing it behind him; and she listened to the muffled conversation happening outside.

"No, no, no, please don't. These men are my guests and have protection in my house. Why don't I bring my daughters out to you instead?" Lot bargained.

The woman gasped. Her husband couldn't possibly dream of putting their girls in the hands of this belligerent mob!

The guests were now near the door, watching the terrified woman trying to determine the best way to shield her daughters from harm. Outside, the crowd beat against the closed door and walls of the house, shouting threats at Lot and clamoring to get to their guests.

Just when the woman thought they would break down the door, the guests inside reached out and pulled Lot in, shutting the door between the family and the unruly crowd. The shouts outside instantly transformed from aggression to confusion and fear.

"I can't see!"

"Why is it so dark?!"

"What kind of sorcery has Lot cast upon us?"

While the men outside fumbled with sudden loss of their sight, the guests spoke with intensity. "Do you have anyone else here with you? Get everyone out of the city because we are going to demolish and obliterate it. God has seen the great wickedness of these people. Time is short, and you must leave to be saved."

Lot's wife watched as her husband ran through the lingering blinded mob to find the two men engaged to his daughters. It wasn't long before he returned without them.

"What happened?" she asked her husband as he slammed the door behind him.

"They didn't believe me!" he exclaimed, wiping his brow. "They refused to come with us!"

By this time, the morning sun was beginning to creep above the plain; and the guests, who had by now revealed themselves to be angels, urgently insisted that the family leave town at once. Lot looked at their comfortable house and at the place that had become home.

In that moment, the angelic strangers grabbed Lot's hand, as well as the hands of his wife and daughters. Together, they ran out of the city, beyond the gates, and into the plain. There, the angels instructed the family to run to the mountains without stopping or looking back because their lives depended on it.

Ever the bargainer, Lot instead persuaded the angels to allow them to escape to another nearby city. With permission, the family raced ahead, hand in hand. Their lungs burned as they gasped for breath, the muscles in their legs beginning to cramp. Yet driven by fear and the angels' urgency, they kept their eyes on the city as it grew closer; and they finally arrived by mid-morning.

By then, God had begun raining down burning sulfur upon Sodom, the only home the woman had ever known. She could smell the fiery destruction; and her heart was full of memories of her beloved streets, her friends, her family, and her freedom. Ignoring the angelic directions, she turned back to the town she loved but could not take another step. Where Lot's wife once stood remained only a pillar of salt.

●●●●●●●●●●●●●●●●●●●●●●●●●●●●●●●●

We never learn Lot's wife's name; and minimal details make it easy to view her as a villain, while teachers frequently make her into an object lesson for all who love something more than the Lord. But a closer look at her heart could reveal more complexities than we often acknowledge. We might recognize more that we have in common with her than we ever expected. Her disobedience had severe consequences, but we can learn from her mistakes and be sure we choose to honor the Lord instead of having divided hearts.

From her, we find that three significant things can change the course of our lives. First, the motivation of our hearts matters. Next, our obedience to God is vital. Finally, how we handle challenges that surround us is extremely important. Each of these is key to choosing our path and will lead us the way God prepared for us, cause us to stray waywardly, or send us running hard in the other direction.

Lot's wife's heart was wholly rooted in Sodom. It's quite likely that she grew up in the wicked city and that her marriage to Lot was arranged by her family, as most marriages were in that time and culture. She lived side-by-side with a man the apostle Peter described as righteous in 2 Peter 2:7-9. He said that Lot's soul was disturbed by the things he witnessed in Sodom, then reassured us that God rescues the righteous and provides an escape from judgmental trials. The tragedy is that God offered Lot's wife such an escape, but she turned away from safety. Her close proximity and committed relationship with a righteous husband was not enough to transform her heart into one that sought the Lord. It's likely that her actions reflected many of Lot's values, but she had yet to internally embrace God's way of life for herself. When presented with the crucial moment to choose between two worlds, her affection for her disintegrating community outweighed everything she knew about the God Who wanted to spare her from destruction.

Before quickly judging her decision, we can consider that she probably didn't long to return to Sodom because of its sinfulness. The city was her familiar home, full of loved ones. Lot's wife watched houses, streets, and precious people being pelted with burning sulfur. She grew up with these people, learned from them, shopped with them, gossiped among them, and helped them when they were sick. They stood by each other through milestones like marriages or losses. Her parents, siblings, extended family, and friends were in agony. Lot's wife's attachment to her city was not completely sinful. However, she accepted the wickedness as part of a package deal, alongside loving her neighbor. In the years she was married to Lot and learned the ways of his God, did she stand up for truth? Was she a champion of compassion? Did she discourage cheating and violence? Or did she chalk it all up to "that's just the way it is" and continue as if it was normal?

We know that Lot's wife divided her heart between a virtuous husband and a culture that defied God. When it came time to make the ultimate decision, she chose what was most dear to her. She knew Who God was, what He commanded, and what His love was like. Yet at the crucial time, she rejected Him. All the complicated values and emotions inside of her drove her back toward a burning city and into the same judgment suffered by her loved ones. Lot's wife teaches us that in the big moments, when decisions must be made quickly, every day-to-day choice comes together to influence what we ultimately decide. This means each moment matters, and our present actions direct our future.

"All a person's ways seem pure to them, but motives are weighed by the LORD," says Proverbs 16:2. This verse reveals God's ability to see straight into our hearts, bypassing our external actions to assess our motivation. It also reminds us that our point of view is not always so clear. Perhaps we can't see the proverbial forest due to the trees, being so wrapped up in our day-to-day struggles as we do our best to make righteous choices. So what do we do to keep our motivations in line with God's holiness?

Romans 8:6 compares living by our human nature to life directed by the Holy Spirit, explaining that "the mind governed by the flesh is death, but the mind governed by the Spirit is life and peace." Though it sounds ominous at first glance, this is good news! It means that we don't have to go it alone because the Holy Spirit is with us and in us, guiding us toward God's way of life and secure peace. While Lot's wife was missing this crucial element, when we are in Christ, we are never abandoned to navigate challenges alone.

That's something to celebrate with gratitude! When we connect with the Holy Spirit and set our motivations on what glorifies God, we can walk away from metaphorical burning cities and the temptations that surround us.

Yes, the motivation of our heart is a big deal, but that's not the final answer. If our heart is seeking righteousness but our actions don't line up with our intentions, we're still in trouble. How often do we find ourselves conflicted when what we read on the pages of God's Word contrasts with the society that surrounds us? We want to love our enemies, but revenge is celebrated. We understand that caring for widows, orphans, and foreigners is an expression of God's love; but once we've earned our money by working hard, we feel that we deserve to benefit from all of it. And resting on the Sabbath seems to be an old-fashioned, optional suggestion. Little by little, our compromising choices can betray our genuine desire to serve the Lord. However, we are called to obedience for a good reason.

Obedience brings glory to God and blesses us in the process. The instructions that God gives us are always for our good, whether to avoid trouble or to experience blessing. His direction leads us step by step from a myriad of seemingly small moments to the big-picture results. And lest we imagine that we exist in isolation, the commands from God affect everyone around us. Family, friends, neighbors, and strangers around the world experience the ripple effect of our obedience. For example, if we follow what Scripture says about tithing, we directly impact the church where we give. Those funds could be used for outreach efforts, providing care to people in our city or across the world. Similarly, responding to God's call to turn the other cheek when in conflict could alter the course of events in our relationship with that person, as well as how they respond to others in their lives. We might not always see the results of our obedience, but it will never be wasted. Ephesians 2:10 declares, "For we are God's handiwork, created in Christ Jesus to do good works, which God prepared in advance for us to do." Ignoring our purpose and missing out on God's goodness would be an incredible tragedy.

Lot's wife was not perfect, and neither are we. But despite her track record, she had the opportunity for another chance, a fresh start outside of a destroyed Sodom. No matter what she chose in the past, in that crucial moment, she could have chosen obedience. Imagine what kind of legacy she could have left! Instead of a pillar of salt, she could've been a pillar in her new community. She had the potential to learn about God's mercy and the way of life He designed for His children. Instead, her disobedience ended in disaster.

Despite the mistakes we've made in the past, we can choose to obey God today. We can rewrite the direction of our current story and allow Him to transform it into something beautiful. Moses told the Israelites, "Walk in obedience to all that the LORD your God has commanded you, so that you may live and prosper and prolong your days in the land that you will possess."[2] We, too, can be encouraged that we will experience blessings when we obey God.

Finally, we must examine our relationship to our environment. Early in Genesis, we find Lot still in the company of his uncle Abram. Their people and livestock had grown to a point where they were too crowded on the same land. Abram allowed Lot to choose where he would live before the two went their separate ways. Lot chose the plains near Sodom because they were well-watered and would support the animals and people. Even then, Scripture notes that the folks in Sodom were living horrible, sinful lives. What looked like good, life-giving land deceptively disguised a troublesome community. It seems that whatever Lot knew about the state of Sodom, he thought he could handle it. He chose material and physical benefits at the expense of moral and spiritual goodness. That was a costly mistake. Thankfully, Lot set his heart on the Lord, allowing him a narrow escape from destruction.

How do we exist in a troubled world without succumbing to temptation ourselves? We align our heart's motivation with the Lord's and keep our feet moving obediently in His direction, constantly seeking Him. Additionally, He gives us discernment so that we can promote His glory in our environment

---

2   Deut. 5:33

instead of allowing our environment to drag us into sin. When Jesus taught about the kingdom of God, He discussed the days of the Son of Man. He likened it to the times of Noah and Lot, when people went about their business and suddenly judgment struck. He said, "Remember Lot's wife! Whoever tries to keep their life will lose it, and whoever loses their life will preserve it."[3]

We may not be in those dramatic days yet, but Jesus also said that the kingdom of God is in our midst. We can certainly remember Lot's wife—her humanity, her intentions, and her mistakes—and then learn to walk with the Spirit. We will live as she couldn't, and our days will be remembered with joy and gladness.

---

3   Luke 17:32-33

CHAPTER 3
Benjamin

Based on Genesis 35-50

Benjamin looked up at his big brother, squinting in the hot Canaanite sun. Maybe later, Joseph would tell him another story or about one of his dreams. The other brothers never wanted to listen, though Benjamin didn't understand why. The dreams were always interesting, even the confusing ones. The older brothers probably also wanted a special robe like the one their father gave Joseph. Benjamin secretly hoped that someday, he would wear something so wonderful. He knew that Father loved Joseph a little extra, though.

Their father used to love someone else the most. Even at a young age, Benjamin was told how Father treasured their mother, the favorite of his four wives. She was beautiful and strong, and everyone said Joseph was so much like her.

Benjamin wished he could remember her. He could only imagine the day he was born, his baby cries joined by her tears. She called him Ben-Oni, "son of my trouble." After she died that day, Father had renamed him Benjamin, "son of my right hand." He was determined that tragedy would not be a lifelong dark cloud over the child.

Father had twelve sons altogether; but his gaze fell mostly on Joseph, who represented the memory of their mother. Joseph was extraordinary. And Benjamin wanted to be just like him.

Benjamin walked with Joseph as he returned from the field where the sheep were grazing. All the brothers were taking care of their flocks; but sometimes, they looked away from the animals to compete against one another to see who was stronger or had better aim at throwing rocks. Joseph thought their father would want to know what was going on beyond his watchful eye, so he kept him informed. This made the brothers furious! But today, they were mad about the dream.

"Tell me again, Joseph?" Benjamin asked.

"We were all putting together sheaves of grain when mine stood up. Then everyone else's grain bowed down to mine. But that wasn't the best dream. Last night, I dreamed that eleven stars, along with the sun and moon, also bowed to me!"

Joseph had a far-away look in his eye, and Benjamin imagined what the glowing heavens must have looked like with Joseph in the center. Even they knew he was special.

The afternoon stretched on as the sun got lower in the sky. Benjamin sighed with boredom as he looked yet again toward the field for any sign of his brothers. He couldn't wait for the days when he'd be free to watch the sheep instead of helping the women at home. Some days, his father would tell a story or walk with him for a little while; and Benjamin loved every minute. Suddenly, Benjamin noticed the women abandoning supper preparations and rushing out of the tents. The brothers were back from the field, and something was wrong!

Voices grew louder, and one brother revealed what was in his hand—Joseph's robe! But it was barely recognizable—ripped, torn, and covered in what looked like blood. Their father began to wail, lamenting for his precious Joseph, who was attacked and eaten by a ferocious beast. The women were crying, and the brothers couldn't even look at one another.

Benjamin tried to hold back tears, barely able to believe that Joseph was never coming back. And what about the wild animal? Were any of them safe? How could such a thing happen? Benjamin watched as their father, with tears streaming down into his beard, tore his own clothes in grief. Would life go on without their beloved Joseph?

Life did resume, but it was never the same. The solemn tension that began the day Joseph died set the tone for the weeks, months, and years to come. Their father spoke often of his favorite son, telling stories to keep his memory alive just as he had with their mother. What would Joseph have become if he had lived beyond his seventeen years? Benjamin hoped Joseph would've been proud of the man he became. Now in his thirties, he had sons of his own. Benjamin couldn't fathom the despair he would feel if even one of them were lost or violently killed like his older brother. He understood his father's deep grief and pitied the elderly man.

His sympathy and respect for their father helped Benjamin navigate his inherited role of favorite son. Immediately after they lost Joseph, new restrictions kept young Benjamin from danger. While he enjoyed his father's affection, Benjamin also longed for the days he could join the others tending sheep. His brothers also spent more time with him, though they never spoke of Joseph. They avoided Benjamin's questions, and he eventually stopped asking.

Over time, their father knew he couldn't confine Benjamin to the tents indefinitely. Though he was permitted to begin shepherding, Benjamin often stayed near the homestead, learning new skills as he helped his father with work. He suspected that the old man feared losing his youngest son as traumatically as he had lost his dearest boy, so Benjamin tried to be patient when he felt smothered or overprotected as an adult. He would do his best to represent the memories of his mother and brother as he felt great love from his father. And so life quietly continued.

Then the famine struck. If only there was more water. Rain became scarce and then stopped altogether. The crops dried, shriveled, turned to dust, and disappeared. Despite careful planning, their provisions ran low. After all the family had been through, would hunger be the beast that overtook them?

Their father clung to the covenant God made with his grandfather, Abraham, generations before. Because of this promise, he didn't believe they would perish in the drought. He had heard that there was food in Egypt, so he sent ten of his sons on the long journey to bring back grain and provide hope for them all. But Benjamin was not permitted to join them.

"It's too dangerous," their father said.

Swallowing his frustration, Benjamin pushed away his excitement at the idea of seeing a new distant land and the adventure of a long journey. After all, his father had seen much in his many years and was probably right. It was too dangerous.

The days of hunger and waiting went on and on. It was a joyful day when the ten brothers finally returned with food to sustain the family, but there was something more. They'd had trouble in Egypt with the high official in charge of the grain supply. He had accused the brothers of being spies! When they had finally left with the provisions they bought, they had made an alarming discovery. During the nighttime rest, they found that the silver they had used to pay for their grain was right there in their sacks. They would be considered swindlers, thieves!

As they told the story, Benjamin realized he only counted nine men. Where was his brother, Simeon?

The situation was worse than he had initially thought. The high official had interrogated the brothers, who had told him about their father and Benjamin. To prove that they were not spies, the official had kept Simeon captive and told the other nine to return to Egypt with Benjamin. This would show that they were telling the truth. Simeon would be free, and they could continue to trade for more food in Egypt.

Benjamin's heart quickened with fear and anticipation. Why was the official so interested in him? And here was the opportunity to go beyond their land and see Egypt! Perhaps it was a blessing in disguise.

Before Benjamin could ask when they would be leaving, their father spoke. "Benjamin will not go to Egypt. Just as Joseph is no more, so we have lost Simeon. Now you want to take my youngest son from me? No, I could not survive if we lost him, too."

And with his silence that followed, they knew his decision was made.

The famine did not relent, and the grain they bought in Egypt could not last forever. Benjamin worried about his family's survival, knowing that their only hope was Pharaoh's food supply. Their situation left Father no choice. He must send his sons back to buy more grain, and that meant risking Benjamin's life. What would the official do to his beloved son? Would he detain him along with Simeon?

The family made a plan. The brothers would take the best gifts they could offer: honey, spices, nuts, and more. They would pay double the amount of silver to make up for the silver that was left in their grain bags. And despite their father's distress, Benjamin would make the journey. His brother Judah personally guaranteed his safety, hoping to reassure their anxious father.

The urgency they felt at being reunited with Simeon and their eagerness to return home with food ignited the pace of the journey. Benjamin observed as many details of the landscape as he could as they hurried on to Egypt.

The long days of travel passed quickly; and soon, they stood at the feet of the high official. Benjamin couldn't help but stare at the man who had summoned him to this new country with its strange customs and unfamiliar language. But within minutes of their arrival, the brothers were whisked away to a house in the palace! His brothers' fear spread to Benjamin's core as they whispered panicked suspicions that they were about to be enslaved as punishment for the silver incident. Reuben bravely stood before the high official's steward and began to explain that they never intended to steal from the palace, but the steward interrupted him.

"It's all right. God gave you the silver; you have paid in full. Do not be afraid," he said calmly.

In the next moment, Simeon emerged and rushed to embrace the brothers. Before they could ask him about his time in captivity, the steward took them inside the high official's house, explained that they would eat with the official himself, and helped them freshen up from their journey. Benjamin wondered if this happened to everyone who visited Egypt; but if that was true, his brothers would not be so tense and worried. Was this a trap? How long would this take? Their family desperately needed grain, and delays would cause more suffering. And what about their father? Would his frail heart be able to withstand the waiting and the worry?

Benjamin was abruptly shaken from his thoughts as the household staff snapped to attention and the high official entered the room. The brothers immediately bowed to the respected man and humbly gave him their gifts from Canaan. The official asked about their father and, once assured that he was still living, turned his attention to Benjamin. With sweaty palms and a pounding heart in his chest, Benjamin barely heard him say something about God's grace before the official suddenly turned and exited the room.

Stunned, the brothers nervously looked at one another, hoping that one of them understood these strange events. Were they safe? Had they offended the Egyptians? Why were they receiving special treatment?

When the high official returned, the meal was served. The men couldn't help but notice that they had been seated in order of their birth. Could this be coincidence, or did Simeon tell them during his imprisonment? How could the Egyptians know their ages?

Benjamin's stomach growled, the aroma of the rich meal colliding with his hunger. His eyes widened when the dishes from the high official's own table were served to them. The meats and vegetables piled high in front of him were five times the size of what filled his brothers' plates. Benjamin was accustomed to his father's favor at home, but did the Egyptians frequently honor the youngest instead of the oldest? Was this another cultural difference? He couldn't help but notice the gaze of the high official throughout the feast, often watching Benjamin as he tried not to satisfy his appetite too quickly. Egypt was a strange place, but Benjamin had forgotten what it was like to be well-fed and full. He silently thanked God for this wild adventure.

Early the next morning, all eleven brothers saddled their donkeys with an abundant supply of newly purchased food. They resumed their urgent pace, this time setting their feet toward Canaan.

Egypt became smaller in the distance behind them when the sound of hoof beats slowed their travel. Benjamin squinted in the sun and recognized the high official's steward galloping their way, shouting at them to stop in the name of Pharaoh! When he caught up with him, his accusation was grave.

"Why have you robbed my master after his kindness to you? You have stolen his personal silver cup after he welcomed you into his own home!"

Alarmed, the brothers fervently insisted that they were innocent, reminding the steward of the silver they had brought to rectify their previous mix-up. They offered their bags to be searched; and the steward declared that the proven thief would be a slave in the high official's house, while the rest would be free to return home. One by one, each of the parcels packed onto the donkeys was thoroughly examined, beginning with Reuben's and once again moving from oldest to youngest. As expected, the cup was not in any of their bags.

Only Benjamin's remained, and he knew he did not have the chalice. He exhaled a sigh of relief as the steward untied his sack, but all air left his lungs as the sunlight glinted off the curved silver cup half-buried in the grain. How could this be? Who had placed the sacred vessel in his bundle? His mouth was dry and his eyes wet with escaping tears. He simultaneously thought of the punishment ahead and the grief of his father, whom he would never see again.

The sounds of his brothers' outrage were muffled as he struggled to maintain focus. The steward led him away, and the other ten followed along with the donkeys.

In what seemed like a heartbeat, they were back in front of the high official. This time, there was no warmth in his voice; and his stare was icy. Bowed low to the ground, Benjamin hoped for even a remnant of the kindness shown to them yesterday from this man who would now rule over him.

Judah, remembering his promise to their father, attempted to negotiate with the official, offering them all as slaves. Benjamin was slightly reassured that his brothers wouldn't quickly abandon him in Egypt. Though what power did they have under this man who was second only to Pharaoh himself?

Judah boldly looked the official in the eye as he told the story of their family, including their father's grief. "If his youngest son does not come home, it will kill him."

Benjamin dared to raise his head from his bowed position and was astonished at what happened next. The high official's face contorted in emotion as he exclaimed that all of his attendants were to leave him alone with the eleven Hebrew men. Tears flowed as he sobbed, bewildering Benjamin and his brothers. Benjamin was uncomfortable at the sudden outburst but felt compassion for the weeping man.

The official's next words startled them all. "It's time to tell you. I'm the brother you sold. I am Joseph!"

Benjamin gasped in disbelief. How did Pharaoh's right hand man know about their dead brother? Why would he claim to be Joseph?

The official continued. Looking straight at Benjamin, he said, "Do not be upset or even furious. God sent me here to help people live through the famine. Return to our father and tell him all that has happened. Then hurry back with the whole family. You can live in nearby Goshen, a beautiful land where you will thrive for many years."

Then Joseph embraced Benjamin tightly, and the reunited brothers cried in one another's arms. Benjamin was overwhelmed with gratitude and amazement that, in an instant, the family's story was transformed from tragedy to miraculous reconciliation. His beloved brother was alive! And a new future was on the horizon.

●●●●●●●●●●●●●●●●●●●●●●●●●●●●●●●●●

Benjamin was born on the sidelines as the joy of his birth was overshadowed by the tragedy of his mother's death. He was the youngest of twelve; and though he was promoted to favored son, the memory of Joseph remained a significant presence. Even in adulthood, Benjamin's place in the family defined his role. He never outgrew the limits and restrictions that were intended to protect him. His life was preserved at the cost of his freedom.

Our family members and our place among them affect so much more than we might realize. Books have been written about the ways birth order influences personality, habits developed during childhood, and beyond. Though we might grow and change, sometimes, our family holds onto the view of us that was established in our youth, never allowing us to expand and mature. We might feel limited like Benjamin, whether from our families' firm action, pervasive attitudes, or emotional responses. After a lifetime of being told who we are, it's easy to believe it ourselves. Before we know it, we find ourselves sidelined by the people closest to us.

Human beings are naturally comparative. We look to others as we attempt to measure and evaluate our status and standards, to figure out where we stand and if we're achieving "enough." Before we realize it, outside opinions hold greater weight than our own. It matters to us what our friends think, how our coworkers perceive us, and if our community approves. This opens the door to further sidelining if we permit other people to define our place in the big picture. Our world is so crowded that it's nearly impossible to avoid feeling swept aside as we lose our true identity in favor of how others view us.

Being limited by others feels bleak and discouraging. But there is good news! Our Creator, the God Who rules the universe, loves us uniquely and specifically. As the One Who made us, He alone has the authority to define us. He says that we are chosen, His children, "handiwork,"[4] "a new creation,"[5] and "fearfully and wonderfully made."[6] These are only a few of the many ways that God describes us, and His Word makes it clear that we are precious to Him. Even when we're deep into sin, our actions don't truly label us. Yes, we are sinners, but we are forgiven and redeemed. Mistakes don't change the fact that we were carefully made in the image of God.

God refuses to be shackled to the limits our families and others place on us. Even in the confines of an overprotective parent, Benjamin had purpose. He was a bridge to reconciliation between Joseph and the brothers who had sold him into slavery. When Joseph reconnected with his youngest brother who did him no wrong, he was able to mend his relationship with the rest of the family. Benjamin could have responded with anger at the deception of Joseph's silver cup scheme, but his heart was soft and willing to embrace his long-lost brother. Benjamin might have allowed this story to have an unhappy ending, but he walked in line with God's purposes. Certainly, his years learning about God from his father influenced Benjamin's reaction. Even while Benjamin was on the sidelines, the Lord was at work.

This family's story didn't end in the palace or even after relocating to the land of Goshen. The descendants of each brother became a tribe of Israel with a complicated history. Benjamin's tribe produced Saul, Israel's first king. The Benjaminites were part of many key battles, as told in the Old Testament. The apostle Paul was also from the tribe of Benjamin.

Digging into the tribe's legacy is complex, and not everything they did was positive. However, we see that Benjamin's influence reached beyond his lifetime. What values did he teach his sons that were then passed down

---

4   Ephesians 2:10
5   2 Corinthians 5:17
6   Psalm 139:14

through generations? How did his family experience shape him as a parent and grandparent? Could the family of Benjamin have valued relationships more? Did they repeat patterns of favoritism and protective guardianship instead of learning from the mistakes of the past? When we realize that our actions today leave a legacy tomorrow, we can take more care to choose what that legacy might be. Our eyes are opened to the significance of our lives, even when we are on the sidelines.

No matter how we fit into our families or how others might try to limit us, we are who God made us to be. Understanding this requires us to look for His direction so that we can find our purpose in Him. That is our route to freedom, and it can happen not only when we are at the front and center of life's action but also when we feel abandoned in the shadows. Even then, our God-given purpose allows us to break free. As we communicate with the Lord, rely on the Holy Spirit, and study His Word, we can see the ways in which He works out the smallest details for our good. Where we once felt trapped might be the exact place where we fulfill His good plans for us.

While we can't deny that others influence our lives, we can remain steadfast in our Heavenly Father's love when we are on the receiving end of someone else's negativity. He gives us strength to step out of the roles that have been assigned to us by others and follow Him instead. With His help, we can overcome the feelings of guilt and obligation that may have developed during our time on the sidelines. He can open our eyes to see how He's using our experience to help us grow, freeing us from the narrative that others created for us. With God's help and design, we can rewrite the story. Like Benjamin, we may have long seasons of waiting or discouragement; but also like Benjamin, we have a history with a God we can trust.

The Lord gives us the opportunity to see things from another perspective. How are we influencing those around us? Who might we be limiting? Who are we encouraging? Jesus invited us to share His love with everyone we encounter, telling us to let our light shine before others so they can see our good deeds and glorify God.[7] Instructions to love one another and descriptions of that love are abundant in Scripture. The potential for our influence to bless those around us is limitless, but we have the responsibility to choose to be that light.

Benjamin's life and legacy might seem to be in the shadow of his famous older brother, but he is no less treasured by our Heavenly Father. No matter what earthly roles we accept, our God sees us individually, uniquely, and as His beloved. Benjamin's purpose was just as significant as Joseph's. While our journeys may take different routes, God has a reason for every step, even those taken from the sidelines.

---

7   Matthew 5:16

CHAPTER 4
Jethro

Based on Exodus 2-4 and 18

He always felt peaceful after rituals. Jethro ambled back to his tent, his thoughts still lingering on the gods. Being connected to something greater than himself brought confidence that everything would be well. Yes, difficulties arose. But Jethro knew that wisdom existed beyond his understanding, and he would continue to seek it while honoring the deities. In turn, they had blessed him with seven daughters, livestock, and the respect of the Midianite people. Jethro was privileged to serve them as a priest.

He also enjoyed the daytime peace as his daughters tended the sheep in the valley. They allowed the flock to graze and then returned home for an evening meal, sharing stories with their father. Jethro delighted them with tales of the past and lessons learned from his own life. Their family enjoyed this regular routine, and they thanked the gods for many blessings.

Jethro was about to step into the welcome shade of the tent when movement in the distance caught his eye. Squinting into the sun, he realized that his daughters were returning with the sheep. It was only midday, which meant something must have gone wrong to drive them back to camp. As they approached, he quickly counted all seven women to be sure they were safe. Sheep could be replaced, but his daughters were each a beloved treasure.

He rushed to greet them and find out why they were home so soon. Excited chatter intensified as Jethro met the shepherdesses.

"There was trouble at the well again today, Father," Zipporah began calmly. She was abruptly interrupted by her sister.

"They wouldn't let us water the sheep!" she exclaimed indignantly. Another daughter was clearly disgusted.

"Those shepherds from the West have no respect and assume that they can overrun us. How can anyone be that selfish?"

Her complaint was cut short as the youngest daughter blurted out, "A good man, an Egyptian, appeared just in time! You should've seen him, Father. He was bold and handsome and spoke with authority. The shepherds almost put up a fight but he persisted, despite being outnumbered!"

Zipporah continued in her typical matter-of-fact manner. "Somehow, he managed to water the flock efficiently. We thanked him and returned home before the shepherds attempted any retaliation."

"Where is he now?" Jethro was alarmed at the lack of hospitality. "Did you leave him at the well? Quick, go invite him to supper before he continues his travels!"

That evening, Jethro repeatedly thanked the kind stranger for rescuing his daughters. The meal ended too quickly, so he invited their guest to remain with them overnight. He learned that this man, Moses, was an Israelite by birth but raised by Pharaoh's family. Moses was escaping trouble and unable to return home, so Jethro welcomed him for as long as he'd like to stay.

A few weeks later, it was clear that Moses had settled into the rhythm of their daily life. Jethro was glad for his presence as a shepherd, ensuring his daughters' safety as they tended the flocks.

After a few months, Moses and Zipporah had become close. It was time to make Moses an official family member, so Jethro arranged their marriage.

Soon, the priest of Midian held grandsons in his arms and thanked the gods for yet another blessing.

His habits became slightly slower as he aged, but his sense of duty to his family and the Midianites remained steadfast. He pondered the wisdom of the gods as he walked to his tent in the late afternoon heat. Zipporah was preparing food in anticipation of Moses' return from the valley later that evening. Neither of them expected the story they were about to hear.

Moses appeared to be both exhilarated and somewhat overwhelmed as he recounted the incredible wonders he had experienced that day. Jethro hung on every word as his son-in-law described a bush that burned but was not consumed and then the voice of Yahweh, the God of the Israelites. Moses explained that God had instructed him to return to Egypt and lead his people to freedom. With a shaky voice, he asked his father-in-law for his blessing to make the journey.

Jethro hesitated for a moment, imagining Zipporah and his grandsons so far away. But the priest knew that the ways of the gods guided them, and Moses' God needed him for a crucial purpose. And so, days later, Jethro watched his dear daughter and son-in-law walk toward the horizon until he could no longer see them. That day, his ritual would include an appeal to *Yahweh* for their safety.

The news from Egypt was astounding, and it reached Midian quickly and regularly. As Pharaoh denied Moses' requests to release the Israelites from bondage, the Lord unleashed terrible plagues upon the people. Frogs, pestilence, boils, and other horrors seemed ineffective to persuade Egypt's ruler. Thankfully, Moses sent Zipporah and their sons back home, where they would be safe from turmoil. The family waited anxiously for each new update, constantly marveling at the strength of *Yahweh*, a God Who cared for His people.

Jethro needed confirmation from multiple people when he heard that Pharaoh had actually agreed to allow the Israelites to leave Egypt. He could barely believe the reports of their escape once Pharaoh regretted losing his workforce of slaves and sent his army after them. The accounts baffled Jethro. *How could something so miraculous be true?* Yahweh controlled the sea, parting the mighty waters to create a secure, dry route to the other side. Not a single Israelite was lost when the waves plummeted back to the seabed, obliterating the Egyptian soldiers, horses, and chariots. No other god had ever done such a thing. Jethro was soon worshiping Yahweh more than any other.

A few short months later, the Midianite priest was eager to reunite with his son-in-law. Together with Zipporah and the boys, they journeyed to meet Moses and the people at their camp near the mountain of God. The enthusiastic reunion included Moses retelling the epic tale of their time in Egypt and the amazing marvels of the Lord. Jethro's soul stirred at the compassionate rescue by this powerful God.

"Praise Yahweh! He is superior to all other gods, and we must honor Him," Jethro exclaimed. He constructed a simple altar and offered sacrifices to the most important God. Then the elders of Israel, including Moses' brother, joined Jethro for a meal in the Lord's presence.

The next day, Jethro proudly watched his son-in-law lead. As the day wore on, Moses was single-handedly responsible for judging matters among all the Israelites. This was entirely too much for one man to handle! Jethro's years of leadership experience had equipped him to manage this situation.

"Moses, this isn't sustainable. You're going to exhaust yourself, but there's a better way," Jethro gently advised. He explained that Moses should still stand before Yahweh for the people and continue as a capable leader, showing the Israelites how to honor God with their lives. However, he needed to appoint honest men who also feared God to serve as judges. They could handle the straightforward cases and reserve only the most challenging dilemmas to Moses. This would meet the needs of the people and allow Moses to tend to the responsibilities of leadership.

Jethro knew that the Israelites were in competent hands as Moses followed this advice. Matters were handled more efficiently, and Moses was able to focus on teaching the people the ways of God. With Yahweh's strength and care, they would journey on to a land of promise. The priest's heart was peaceful as he returned home to Midian. From now on, he would give praise and honor to the Most High God.

●●●●●●●●●●●●●●●●●●●●●●●●●●●●●●●●●●

So much happens in Exodus that it's easy to rush through Jethro's story. But as he provided Moses with helpful advice, he offers us the opportunity to learn as well. Our introduction to Jethro showcases hospitality. Whether out of gratitude, tradition, or the obligation of social custom, he extends kindness to Moses. His welcome demonstrates acceptance of foreign strangers. It also foreshadows the parable Jesus told in Luke 14. He instructs those present at a shared meal that when they are hosting a banquet, they are not to invite friends, relatives, or rich neighbors. Instead, they are to welcome the poor, the disabled, and those who cannot repay the gesture—and they will be blessed.

Being on the sidelines presents us with a golden occasion to offer hospitality. Our generous, unconditional kindness can change someone's story for the better. Imagine if Jethro left Moses at the well or sent him on his way with gifts and gratitude. Or what if they said farewell after the initial supper and Moses continued to wander? Instead, the security of a loving family surely helped shape Moses' character. Witnessing Jethro as Midian's priest was the beginning of the training that Moses would need when he stepped into his own leadership position. He certainly learned something about shepherding the Israelites while tending literal flocks. Jethro's invitation to Moses was much more than dinner. He impacted Moses' life with lasting effects.

We, too, have Jethro's gift of welcoming, should we choose to share it. Small gestures or long-term care can positively affect someone and produce lasting goodness in their life. A glass of water to the thirsty, a meal to the hungry, or a blanket to the cold are simple ways to practice this. Opening our homes for an evening or extended stay, like Jethro did, can provide a safe environment for the weary to rest. Sharing our stories and skills can be a blessing and giving the unconditional love of God will always encourage a heart.

Despite how we sometimes feel, we are not weak or incapable when we are on the sidelines. We have the power to support someone else as they pursue God's design for them. Simultaneously, we fulfill His intent for us as well. We aren't running on individual tracks with compartmentalized purposes. God weaves a tapestry, with the threads of our lives intertwining with one another. Sometimes, His plans for each of us overlap; and we work together, journey together, and offer encouragement together. Moses may have been front and center when leading the Israelites out of Egypt, but Jethro's smaller role was equally significant from God's point of view. The Lord is intentional with every detail; and Jethro, from Midian, was part of His plan to free His people. The possibilities are limitless when we consider how our piece of the puzzle helps complete the big picture.

Jethro also demonstrated purposeful wisdom. His thoughtful decision to arrange Zipporah and Moses' marriage added a hard-working shepherd to the family. Exodus 18 highlights Jethro's administrative wisdom and gentle, effective guidance as Moses implemented his plan to delegate duties. Ultimately, the recognition of the supreme holiness and authority of God, despite a polytheistic background, reveals the most about Jethro's wisdom. All wisdom comes from the only true God, though it took the Midianite quite some time to realize and understand this.

There is an endless supply of such wisdom available to us today. The same God who led the Israelites to freedom is leading us, too. Proverbs 2:6 says it plainly: "For the Lord gives wisdom; from his mouth come knowledge and understanding." Not only are we loved by the source of all wisdom, but He also gladly gives it when we seek Him. We are reassured that "if any of you lacks wisdom, you should ask God, who gives generously to all without finding fault, and it will be given to you."[8]

The Lord leads us through experiences and observations to help us grow in knowledge with discernment. This wisdom is not intended to be kept for ourselves. Especially when we feel like we're in the background, we have the opportunity to share our God-given insight and encourage others to see where the Lord is leading them. This is by design; God made us to need each other and utilize our differences to work together. Paul illustrated this with the imagery of one body made up of many parts. The foot is not like the hand or the eye, but all are necessary for the body to function. The same is true for the body of Christ.[9] And while we may think that some people are more important than others, that's not the case! When we're working together, there is often not a central leader. Rather, a group of equals, who might all mistakenly feel less significant, unite to complete God's kingdom work. But what a difference it makes to see ourselves through God's eyes! Jethro's guidance helped Moses see that; and though Moses remained God's chief shepherd of the Israelites, the gifts of his helpers benefited everyone.

Obtaining and sharing wisdom is a large part of our sidelines purpose. Additionally, we have the gift of perspective. Moses had so much to see and process. His background, place in a new land, family life, and work as a shepherd were plenty to carry. But then he received a miraculous calling from God with a larger mission than anything he'd ever known. That's a lot to take in; and likely, he had difficulty working through it all. Jethro, however, saw from a little more distance, outside of Egypt and the Israelite community. He was a spectator to Moses' experiences. The result was that Jethro was able to support and encourage Moses, further equipping him for the task to which God called him.

---

8   James 1:5
9   1 Corinthians 12:15-27

When we are a few steps away from the action, what can we see that others might miss when they have a figurative spotlight shining in their eyes? How can our own perspective offer something unique and possibly vital? We have the ability to help others succeed as they, in turn, bless others. We would be mistaken to believe that this role has any less value than that of the people we encourage. We're never inferior but are simply serving in a different way. Often, we're able to offer help in ways that others cannot. In God's reality, there is no hierarchy based on worth. Each beloved child has something to contribute.

When we find ourselves in seasons that leave us feeling less necessary, we must open our eyes to the treasured gifts God has given us. Then, we need to recognize that those gifts were never meant to be kept to ourselves. The joy of sharing and participating in the Lord's work produces blessing upon blessing. Before we know it, we are giving glory to God! Jethro invited Moses into his family; then Moses invited Jethro into the love of the one true God. May our own hospitality, wisdom, and unique perspective do likewise.

CHAPTER 5
Caleb

Based on Numbers 13–14, Joshua 14–15, and the story

of the Israelites in Exodus and Deuteronomy

Freedom still felt strange. Caleb had only known slavery in Egypt, where he was trapped each day in back-breaking work dictated by Pharaoh's demands. Now, the hot sun often revived those vivid memories, but each mile through the dusty wilderness led to new life. The Hebrew people were headed to a land promised by God. Caleb's faith in the Lord grew as his footsteps crunched on the rocky ground. His mind could barely comprehend recent events; one act of God followed by another made it impossible for Caleb to doubt that the Lord was leading them to freedom beyond their imaginations.

Not long ago, Moses had arrived in Egypt with God's commands for Pharaoh to release His people. Caleb witnessed the plagues and Pharaoh's anger, then carefully followed God's instructions as they prepared to leave. Suppressing disbelief, he walked away from days of brickmaking as Moses led them through a dry path in the middle of a parted sea. God directed them by a massive cloud and fire in the sky. When they were thirsty, He gave them water. When their stomachs felt empty, He provided manna and quail.

Caleb joined his brothers in battles, and they were victorious with the Lord's help. They received laws to guide daily life and holy justice when they rebelled, as they did when worshiping an idol of a golden calf. Moses directed them with God's guidance, as he met with the Lord regularly on the mountain. Therefore, Caleb trusted Moses and tried his best to lead his own tribe by that example. The wilderness was difficult; but he followed the way of God, knowing that the Promised Land was just ahead.

Today, he reported to Moses by special request. Twelve men stood expectantly side-by-side, one leader from each tribe. Caleb, representing the tribe of Judah, nodded silently at his friend Joshua of the tribe of Ephraim. They listened eagerly as Moses spoke.

"The Lord directed me to send you up into the hills to scout the land. Find out what the people are like. What are their strengths? How many are there? Learn about their towns and fields. If you can, bring back some of their crops. Then tell us about the place God is giving us."

Caleb was ready for this quest, honored to be chosen to help them get closer to the Promised Land. After accepting their assignment, the twelve returned to their tents to pack for the journey. The Israelites were counting on them to complete this mission.

For forty days, the twelve explored; and what they discovered was incredible. They took in the sights of the land as they traveled from the desert to Hebron, where they observed the descendants of Anak who were tall, strong, and intimidating. Then they moved on to the Valley of Eshkol, which was fertile and abundant! So this is what was meant by a "land of milk and honey." Some used the phrase to describe fertile soil and a place where both livestock and crops could thrive.

The Israelite scouts gathered grapes, pomegranates, and figs, then refreshed themselves in cool streams of water. The size of the grape clusters presented a challenge. How could they transport such unbelievably large, plump fruit? One man suggested that they tie the branch to a pole, which proved successful as they carried their bounty back to the Israelite camp in the wilderness.

As soon as they arrived at their community, Caleb was eager to share their report with Moses, Moses' brother Aaron, and the rest of the people. If only they could've seen the wonders in the valley! He would do his best to describe each detail. Certainly, they would begin their journey to their new home soon, and Caleb was sure that every Israelite looked forward to the day when their feet could rest from travel and settle into new dwellings.

The noise of the crowd grew louder as they stared at the ripe grapes dangling from the pole. Moses quieted the people and welcomed the scouts, thanking them for their willingness to venture out and inviting them to share their findings.

Gaddiel, of the tribe of Zebulun, spoke first. "We scouted out the land as you requested, and yes, it is a place of milk and honey as we've heard! But the current inhabitants are incredibly strong, and they live in large, securely guarded cities. We even saw the Anakites there, towering over us like giants! This place is full of people!"

Caleb did not expect the report to take this direction. Why was Gaddiel focusing on those people? Nine other scouts nodded in agreement with grave expressions, though Caleb saw Joshua shake his head and struggle to speak. Grumbles emerged from the people as they considered that moving into the Promised Land might be more hazardous than they had previously believed.

The murmurs began to crescendo, and Caleb couldn't restrain himself any longer. Looking directly at Moses, he declared, "We should go inhabit this land. It's possible! Remember how God led us in every battle—"

Before he could finish, the other scouts interrupted, passionately disagreeing with Caleb.

Gaddiel spoke again. "No. We absolutely *cannot* attack them. They are far too powerful for us! And they're huge! We're practically bugs compared to them. We would walk into our own destruction!"

The noise from the community rose again as the ten dissenting scouts began answering questions and spreading discouragement through the crowd. Some people began crying; others began shouting insults at Moses and Aaron. This was growing out of control. Their exclamations overlapped each other as order fell apart.

"Why is the Lord taking us somewhere to die?"

"We might as well have just died in Egypt."

"Or why not right here, in this wild land?"

"Our families will be taken from us!"

"We're better off back with Pharaoh!"

"Yes! Moses had his chance. Who will lead us back to safety? To our normal lives?"

Suddenly, Moses and Aaron fell face down on the ground. Caleb and Joshua were so overwhelmed that they could only tear their clothing to express their grief until Caleb pleaded with the people.

"The land that we explored is more than bountiful. With God's favor, He will lead us to that fertile and pleasant country! He will surely grant this to us."

Joshua interjected. "Do not defy the Lord! And don't be afraid of the people, because they aren't protected, while God is on our side. Please, do not let fear fill your hearts."

Caleb's eyes widened as he noticed a few men in the crowd picking up large stones. Would he and Joshua lose their lives tonight, here in this assembly? Should they run and escape before this turned into a riot?

Abruptly, the glory of the Lord appeared at the tent of meeting, a place where Moses met with God. The entire community fell silent as Moses entered to talk with the Lord. Their fears of the new land were replaced by the dread of God's wrath if they disobeyed Him again.

The longer that Moses spoke to God, the more uneasy the Israelites became. Finally, he emerged from the tent to address the troubled people.

"The Lord has spoken. He will not destroy you, even though you are wayward and disobedient. Instead, He has forgiven you. However, not one of you doubting people will see the land of His promise. No one who has treated the Lord with disdain will ever enter that place."

A wave of muffled cries rippled through the crowd. Caleb thought they might become more upset, but Moses continued. "But there are two who will walk into that land. Caleb has chosen differently and follows the Lord with his whole heart. The Lord sees you, Caleb. You will enter the Promised Land, and your descendants will also live there. Joshua, you, too, will enter God's into promise. But the rest of you will spend the rest of your lives in this wilderness, and the next generation will receive this home that God will provide. For the next forty years, you will face the consequences of your sins against God."

Their cries turned into despair. Caleb could only sit in stunned silence. This changed everything.

The next forty years were hard. Whenever it seemed they might settle somewhere, they had to move on again. The decades were long and marked by restlessness, full of conflict and discomfort. Yet they were also full of the joys of everyday life. Caleb delighted in his wife and children. God was there, always providing, and His presence never left them. He still gave them victory in battles.

Meanwhile, despite witnessing the Lord's sovereign power, the Israelites still attempted rebellions. The idea that Egypt held a better life persisted. People grew old; and the stubborn generation began to die, either from natural causes or as a direct result of disobedience to the Lord.

Moses faithfully guided them with God's wisdom, but even he had moments that lacked trust. After disobeying instructions while God amazingly brought water from a rock, Moses learned that he wouldn't enter the Promised Land, either. Joshua, who had been Moses' aide for many years, was chosen to be the next leader of the Israelites. He stepped into command on the day that Moses died.

Caleb continued to serve the tribe of Judah quietly, always demonstrating faithfulness to God. As time passed, God gave the people specific commands about their new home. Caleb was appointed as one of twelve to assign parts of the land to each tribe. Soon, they were finally ready.

The Jordan River was the only thing that separated the Israelites from the Promised Land. Caleb remembered when they stood on the banks of the Red Sea, more than four decades earlier. At that time, they felt the danger of Pharaoh's army pursuing them. Now, they had hope. The new generation watched with wonder as the river stopped flowing, creating a path for them to cross. Each one stepped onto the dry riverbed and walked toward a new freedom, a land flowing with milk and honey.

It wasn't instantly peaceful; but instead, the next five years included difficult battles as they followed the Lord.

One day, Caleb approached Joshua. "Remember what the Lord said forty years ago? He promised that the very land that I explored would be given to me and my family because I obeyed Him completely. Today, I am eighty-five years old! But I'm still as able as I was those many years ago, so please give me the hills of Hebron. I'm prepared to face the Anakites by the power of God, just as we testified that day in front of the assembly."

With Joshua's blessing, Caleb brought his people into that country; and they were victorious over the same people that the Israelites had feared long ago. Soon, the land saw peace; and Caleb's descendants inherited it, just as God had declared. Caleb, a man with a different spirit who followed the Lord wholeheartedly, helped bring his people home.

● ●

It's easy for us to forget Caleb when we read the long, complex narrative of the Israelites. Though he receives a brief mention, our attention is usually captivated by Joshua's courage. Yet God saw Caleb and knew him well. He didn't overlook His faithful servant; but God was intimately familiar with Caleb's heart, loved him, and constantly covered him with His nurturing hand.

When we gaze at Caleb through God's perspective, we see active, deeply rooted faith. Of course, Caleb was an ordinary person, which gives the rest of us ordinary people hope that we too can live such a dedicated life. With the help of the Holy Spirit, we learn from Caleb's example. He teaches us how to handle pressure, doubt, and fear.

Going against the crowd is extremely difficult, and being different is often a red flag that something could be wrong. We think that we must be making a mistake and everyone else has already figured out the correct answer. Yet Caleb shows us that this is not always the case. We might have heard it said that "what is right is not always popular, and what is popular is not always right." The Israelite scouts demonstrated this proverb with tragic results.

So how do we maintain godly character under pressure? How do we make sure we're doing the right thing in the face of opposition when we go against the crowd? First, we confirm that we are walking with the Lord and being led by the Spirit. Are we in line with God's Word? Proverbs 3:5-6 emphasizes the importance of His ways over ours: "Trust in the Lord with all your heart and lean not on your own understanding; in all your ways submit to him, and he will make your paths straight."

The Israelites trusted in their own limited understanding and cast aside God's instructions. They knew that the Lord had promised them a home in a land flowing with milk and honey. They witnessed tangible proof of His great power and compassionate care for them. However, they didn't understand how His promises would happen; so they allowed skepticism, doubt, and fear to take the lead. This was a disaster, and we can learn from their grave mistake.

After prayerful consideration, when we know we are within God's will, we can step out in faith. Be assured that following God is never in vain. As Paul encouraged, "Let us not become weary in doing good, for at the proper time we will reap a harvest if we do not give up."[10] It takes perseverance to

---

10   Galatians 6:9

stay focused, but we're not left to our own abilities. Jesus explained that the Holy Spirit helps us. He said, "'If you love me, keep my commands. And I will ask the Father, and he will give you another advocate to help you and be with you forever—the Spirit of truth. The world cannot accept him, because it neither sees him nor knows him. But you know him, for he lives with you and will be in you.'"[11] The Lord provides the strength to endure opposition. We do not stand alone.

The believers in the early church lived this reality as extreme persecution threatened the Christ-followers. Peter wrote to these Christians as they encountered danger daily. He asked who would harm them if they were eager to do good and advised that suffering for what is right results in blessing. Peter encouraged them not to be afraid, but to be prepared always to give the reason for hope in Jesus to anyone who asks. But they should do this with gentle respect because it's better, if it's God's will, to suffer for good rather than evil.[12]

Yes, as Peter pointed out, doing the right thing while others do not isn't easy. We'll likely suffer for a while, as Caleb did when he faced derision from his neighbors, who nearly stoned him. Then, he endured forty years of desert wandering because of the community's disobedience, which could have easily inspired resentment or bitterness. But in God's timing, Caleb received his blessing. Additionally, he has an eternal heavenly reward, forever with the One he loved with his whole heart. We, too, will encounter difficulty. However, the encouragement of God's promised blessings can help us continue to follow Him, even when everyone around us is going another way.

Caleb spent his entire life serving God, leading his people, and working diligently alongside his friend, Joshua. Yet as their story unfolded, Joshua's role was elevated to the spotlight—then and now. Each man gave his whole heart to the Lord, yet one received acclaim and the other an honorable mention. This might seem unbalanced and unfair.

---

11   John 14:15-17
12   1 Peter 3:13-17

In our attention-loving society, we are often validated by positive affirmations. Recognition for our efforts encourages us to continue striving for constant improvement, but we become discouraged when no one notices our work. It becomes especially frustrating when others receive more credit than we do, despite equal contributions to a project. How would we feel in Caleb's position? His story helps us navigate through our discouragement by shifting our perspective.

Using accolades as a measurement of our success leads to trouble. Not only is it an inaccurate indicator, but it also encourages us to seek selfish ambition more than accomplishing the task at hand. Eventually, we forget the true reason we are doing something, and congratulations become our motivation. This is an age-old problem that Jesus addressed. In his banquet parable, He advised his followers not to sit in a place of honor but, instead, to humbly choose a seat that indicates less esteem. This would result in one of two possibilities. Either the host could encourage them with an upgraded position; or at least, the guest would be saved from the shame of being demoted to another place at the table.[13]

Humility is a Christ-like quality. Jesus engages this subject again in Matthew 6:2-4:

> So when you give to the needy, do not announce it with trumpets, as the hypocrites do in the synagogues and on the streets, to be honored by others. Truly I tell you, they have received their reward in full. But when you give to the needy, do not let your left hand know what your right hand is doing, so that your giving may be in secret. Then your Father, who sees what is done in secret, will reward you.

We can rest in knowing that God will handle our outcomes so we can focus on truly loving our neighbor and helping in their time of need.

---

13 Luke 14:7-11

When we look at Caleb, we see a man investing his whole self into serving God, trusting that he would live in the Promised Land. He patiently waited until he was eighty-five years old before pursuing his earthly reward. There is no doubt that such a faithful servant would have been prayerful before approaching Joshua about receiving the land. Although Caleb didn't receive as much acclaim as Joshua, he did receive God's blessing. He kept his focus on the Lord and his priorities in focus.

When we are no longer concerned with acknowledgment and credit for ourselves, the glory goes to God, Who truly deserves it. God's kingdom work is truly our motivation and delight, the fulfillment of our purpose. Caleb did not lead the Israelites to receive fame or popularity. He served the God He loved as he cared for the people.

The apostle Paul also described this purpose-focused attitude as he was imprisoned for preaching the gospel. In Philippians, he explained how his time in chains actually furthered the Good News of Christ as he was able to reach more people and demonstrate his faith in powerful ways. Meanwhile, there were others who preached about Jesus for selfish reasons. Paul pointed out that what truly mattered was that the people were hearing the Word of God and the truth of their salvation through Christ.[14]

Of all the people who might notice our achievements, the only eyes that matter are God's. When the Lord looked upon Israel, He didn't merely see a mass of people. Instead, He knew each Israelite personally. God truly saw Caleb, and He pays close attention to us, too. David sings a beautiful song to a God who knows us intimately: "You have searched me, LORD, and you know me. You know when I sit and when I rise; you perceive my thoughts from afar. You discern my going out and my lying down; you are familiar with all my ways. Before a word is on my tongue you, LORD, know it completely. You hem me in behind and before, and you lay your hand upon me."[15] We're never

---

14   Philippians 1:12-18
15   Psalm 139:1-5

overlooked but constantly recognized by the most Important One Who sees and loves us.

Caleb also shows us that faith in God can overcome our anxiety over frightening circumstances. Often, we believe that bravery is a bold absence of fear. However, it might be more accurate to describe it as boldly stepping out in the presence of fear. And as we've learned, we are never alone; the Holy Spirit enables us to be brave. He reminds us of the truths we learned in safer times so that, like David, we can say, "When I am afraid, I put my trust in you. In God, whose word I praise—in God I trust and am not afraid. What can mere mortals do to me?"[16]

Caleb remembered God's words and also what He had done in the past. With every reason to trust the Lord, Caleb courageously stood firm, despite any fear of the people in the Promised Land or of the outrage of the Israelites. He, along with Joshua and the people, was encouraged by Moses' words as they finally prepared to move into God's land: "Be strong and courageous. Do not be afraid or terrified because of them, for the LORD your God goes with you; he will never leave you nor forsake you."[17]

But we might not always feel God near, so He tells us to talk to Him. Communication with our Heavenly Father is key when we're afraid so that He can help us handle our increasing anxiety. In his letter to the Philippians, Paul described our approach as persistent prayer that includes thanksgiving. We'll then receive the peace of Christ, which we can't manufacture on our own and which defies our human understanding. He also encouraged us to think about whatever is excellent and praiseworthy, focusing on things of God.[18] Faith involves looking in the right direction, so we must steady our gaze on our Sovereign Lord to avoid being distracted by lesser things that increase our fear.

Eventually, Caleb helped the Israelites cross the Jordan River into the Promised Land. Decades after firmly opposing a violent, doubting crowd, he

---

16   Psalm 56:3-4
17   Deuteronomy 31:6
18   Philippians 4:6-8

led the people into God's blessing. We can follow Caleb's lead, too. We can be brave in the presence of God while standing confidently on His truths. We can remember our true motivation; and without the distraction of human acclaim, God can use us to influence His people to walk His way. There's more at stake than a personal reward. We have a purpose from the Lord, and it includes serving Him humbly with our whole heart.

CHAPTER 6
Eliab

Based on 1 Samuel 16-17, 22 and 1 Chronicles 27

"**S**top what you're doing and get ready!"

Eliab spun around to find his father, Jesse, out of breath but smiling. Something big must have happened, big enough to inspire the elderly man to sprint from his tent. Eliab continued working while he waited for an explanation. As the oldest son, he had become his father's right hand man, gaining increasing responsibility for the household and livestock. Anything that Jesse asked was promptly completed, and Eliab would naturally become head of the family when the day of his inheritance arrived. But at this moment, he looked at Jesse with confusion and curiosity.

"Samuel is here and has summoned us!" Jesse proclaimed.

Eliab was baffled. "The priest? Why has he come to Bethlehem?"

"To make a sacrifice—and we're invited to attend. Quickly now! Gather your brothers and purify yourselves. We must be prepared promptly. This is an extremely special occasion."

Eliab could sense the urgency in his father's voice and was immediately obedient. They would need to bathe themselves and wash their clothes to be presentable before the Lord, and Samuel might even consecrate them with a special oil. This was the kind of thing that happened in Jerusalem—not in Bethlehem.

By the time they reached the place of the sacrifice, Eliab learned that Samuel's visit was about much more than a routine holy ritual. The Lord had led him here to anoint a new ruler to replace King Saul! Eliab willed his heart to stop pounding so fiercely, but he knew his life was about to change. As the oldest son, he took on new responsibilities and received honor before his brothers. His entire life had been a lesson in leading, producing skills beyond his brothers' capabilities. And he looked like a king—tall, handsome, and self-assured. It all made sense. So when the family arrived for the sacrifice, Eliab wasn't surprised as Samuel made his way towards him.

Then abruptly, the priest halted. He glanced at Jesse and subtly shook his head. What was happening? In disbelief, Eliab allowed Jesse to pull him back while his younger brother, Abinadab, stepped forward. Eliab was baffled. How would Abinadab handle a throne? In a split second, he no longer had to wonder. Samuel passed over his brother and looked to the next oldest, Shammah.

"No, he is not chosen by the Lord, either," Samuel softly declared.

Seven of Jesse's sons were introduced to Samuel, and none of them were approved by the Lord. Perhaps there was a mistake. Could the new king be from a different family or a different town?

The attending elders were still, and Samuel spoke from the silence. "Do you have any other sons?"

David. We forgot about David. In the excitement at the honor of attending the sacrifice, they had left their youngest brother out in the field with the flock. Now Samuel explained that the entire holy ritual would wait until David was brought in to join them.

Eliab's heart once again thumped in his chest but this time with the outrage of injustice. He didn't understand what defect disqualified him from a destiny that, less than an hour ago, he could clearly imagine. This interest in his kid brother—a grimy, immature shepherd—was troubling. Surely, Eliab was more qualified than David!

Time seemed to simultaneously crawl slowly and fly with the speed of a hawk. The wait for David was finally broken by the crowd's murmur when the teen walked in, bewildered and overwhelmed.

Eliab watched in disbelief as Samuel nodded and poured oil from a horn onto David's head, declaring him the next king of Israel. Surrounded by his older brothers, David appeared to have a calm acceptance of his transformed future. Yet Eliab's heart burned with the hot flames of jealousy.

The stench of the battlefield was no longer noticeable after so many weeks at war, if you could call it that. King Saul's army camped on the edge of a valley that separated them from the enemy, but there was no glorious victory or even a rough skirmish. Instead, the days were filled with sweaty, anxious soldiers and lingering smoke from the small fires where they cooked meager amounts of food. Eliab dreaded the daily routine. Each morning and evening, the Philistine army sent their terrifying brute, Goliath the champion, to roar enraged taunts at the quivering Israelites. Today was no exception.

Saul's men dutifully followed their orders to assemble on the front lines. Cries of battle rang out without confidence. They knew they wouldn't fight the Philistines today, and anxiety set the stage for Goliath's daily demands.

"Eliab!"

That familiar annoying voice grated Eliab's exhausted nerves as his scrappy youngest brother emerged from the crowd of assembling soldiers.

"What are you doing here?" Eliab asked through gritted teeth.

"Father sent food for you, Abinadab, and Shammah. And he wants to know what's happening. Have you been fighting? Have you seen anything horrible? How many men have you taken out? What about . . ."

David's incessant questions were stunned into silence by the bone-chilling yell thundering through the valley. There in the distance, but entirely too near for Eliab's liking, stood Goliath in full armor, towering over the trembling Israelites.

"Preparing for battle again? Why bother? Today, I dare you to choose your best warrior and send him to me! We'll fight to the death! Should he succeed, we shall be your servants. But when I pulverize him into dust, Israel shall serve the Philistines for generations to come! Today, I stand against Israel's army!"

With his final battle cry, the men surrounding David and Eliab fled in fear, as they had at the beginning and end of each previous day. They would never grow accustomed to the terror of Goliath of Gath. Eliab grabbed David by the arm and dragged him back to camp. The army buzzed with talk of their enemy.

"Did you see how tall he was? Like a giant!"

"He keeps coming, defying Israel. He'll never relent if we don't do something."

"Someone needs to step up. Save us and then be rewarded by the king!"

"I heard that King Saul will grant riches and honor to the victor who slays Goliath."

"I heard that the hero will marry the king's daughter and his whole family will be given special privileges."

"Who does this Philistine think he is that he defies the living God and His armies?"

David's question caused a sudden silence that seemed to echo across the camp. All eyes were on Eliab's scrawny baby brother. Eliab wanted to clamp his hand over David's mouth; but the other men were actually answering the kid, explaining what would happen if an Israelite could kill the Philistine behemoth. Eliab couldn't hold back his anger any longer and jerked David away from the crowd.

"Why are you here? And who is watching our sheep? Did you just abandon them to fend for themselves in the wilderness?" Eliab's fury grew with every word he spat out. He continued before David could answer. "You've been arrogant and proud ever since the day Samuel came. You think you're special because you occasionally serve in King Saul's courts. But I know who you really are. I know how dark your heart is. You only came here because you wanted to watch real men fight a bloody battle!"

David looked up at his older brother in defiance. "What did I do? You won't even let me say anything!" He turned sharply and rejoined the other men. Eliab watched him disappear into the crowd and marched in the opposite direction. If the little twerp thought he belonged in an army camp, let him fend for himself.

It took most of the day for Eliab's anger to subside, but it was soon replaced by the persistent fear of Goliath's threats. How long would he continue his tirades before the Philistine army pursued them? Eliab tried to focus on not running away as the fierce champion bellowed. Then an all-too-familiar voice rang out from the Israelite army.

"Hey!"

What in the world is David doing here? Eliab's thoughts and heart raced. *Why now? He is going to get himself killed! Well, maybe that would solve some problems. But he'll probably get us all killed!*

Then David stepped out of the crowd and walked steadily toward the massive warrior. He had no protection—only his staff and sling, as if he were protecting his sheep from a predator. Eliab was frozen in place. He wanted to cry out, to pull his brother back to safety. Sure, he couldn't stand the kid, but he didn't want him to die. Yet David kept going.

Everything seemed to happen in slow motion. Eliab could barely register the exchange between the Israelite boy and the Philistine beast. The deep voice of Goliath rumbled with more taunts as David declared victory in the name of the Lord of Israel. Then Goliath lunged forward, and a cry caught in Eliab's throat. *This couldn't be happening! Why didn't David run away?*

Instead, Eliab's little brother raced toward the enemy of Israel, reached into his bag, and grabbed a stone. In one swift, smooth movement, he whirled the sling expertly through the air, releasing the stone just in time to avoid

Goliath's attack. Eliab watched the rock hit the giant's head, knocking their tormentor face down in front of a simple teenage shepherd.

David wasn't done. He grabbed the Philistine's sword and used it to cut off the fallen warrior's head, as if he was a seasoned fighter! Eliab stood in shock as his fellow soldiers rushed past him, pursuing the retreating Philistines at top speed. He couldn't think about David now. He was part of King Saul's army, and they had a war to win.

No one cared about the brother of a champion. No one noticed as Eliab loyally served in King Saul's military while all eyes were on David, the rising star. After the triumphant victory over Goliath, the shepherd boy became a war hero. He lived in the palace, served the king, achieved victory in battle, and married into the royal family. Eliab couldn't ignore his neighbors' boasts about their hometown celebrity or the accolades coming from all over Israel; some of their praise for David even exceeded their cheers for Saul. This, of course, did not please the king. Jealousy developed into murderous rage; and soon, David was running for his life.

Eliab had a choice. No amount of resentment towards his brother would protect him if Saul decided to threaten David's family. And the fact remained that David had been anointed as Israel's future king. Eliab's time in Saul's army had come to an end, and news of David's path of escape made its way back to their father Jesse's household in Bethlehem. After much discussion, their family joined David in hiding, along with four hundred other men who looked to him from their distress, burden of debts, or general discontentment. These men became David's army, fighting with him as he eluded Saul, then growing in number with David's success in battle and his increasing political prominence.

By the time David became king, Eliab took his place as head of their family, as well as of the tribe of Judah. Many men were celebrated with prestige and honor for their service in David's army, but Eliab's name was rarely mentioned. Though he wasn't recognized for victory in battle, he overcame furious envy and made peace with his youngest brother to fight by his side.

●●●●●●●●●●●●●●●●●●●●●●●●●●●●●●●●●

David's riveting story captivates us from the moment he meets Samuel to his last breath, yet Eliab is quickly acknowledged and discarded. After all, the Lord didn't need him on the throne; and he antagonized brave young David. Scripture doesn't tell us anything about Eliab's childhood nor of his accomplishments on the battlefield. We don't know how he led Judah or even his own family. However, we can be sure that though the Lord did not choose Eliab to be Israel's king, He most certainly did not overlook him.

God watched Eliab from birth and knew him completely. He saw his strength, good looks, and developing leadership skills. Jesse and Samuel recognized these traits, too. Perhaps the rest of the community observed them as well as they witnessed Eliab's growth since his childhood. What no human could see was that the Lord was closely watching Eliab's heart, and He knew who Jesse's oldest son would grow up to be.

Our vision is limited. We do our best to understand the people around us; but without Divine intervention, we're unable to comprehend what's in the depths of their hearts. As a result, we apply judgment only by what we can see. The problem is this often leads us away from what God is doing in and among us. When we fail to recognize God's work in our lives, it's difficult to follow Him.

We must seek God's vision, not only as we perceive other people but also as we examine ourselves. The importance of that is vividly illustrated as Samuel met Eliab and discerned God's choice for the next king. "But the LORD said to Samuel, 'Do not consider his appearance or his height, for I have rejected him. The LORD does not look at the things people look at. People look at the outward appearance, but the LORD looks at the heart.'"[19]

---

19   1 Samuel 16:7

We aren't specifically told what was happening within Eliab's soul, but we know that he was not prepared to follow God and lead Israel. David's priorities, however, were in stark contrast to his brother's; and he's often described as a man after God's own heart. This lifelong pursuit of the Lord rings out from Psalm 51 with David's plea for God to make his heart clean and his spirit steadfast. He passed this wisdom down to his son Solomon, who wrote, "A person may think their own ways are right, but the Lord weighs the heart."[20]

Generations later, Jesus taught us that the pure in heart are blessed and will see God. His disciple Peter instructed the early Christians that beauty doesn't come from outward appearance. Instead, God prizes "a gentle and quiet spirit."[21] That's beautiful to Him.

As we pray for insight into God's point of view, we can love others as He loves them; and we can seek His priorities for ourselves. Thankfully, the Lord doesn't keep this a secret or abandon us to figure it out alone. We've been given the gift of His Word, which provides guidance as we shift our focus from ourselves to pursuing God's heart as David did. Eliab demonstrated that our earthly priorities can distract us, causing us to neglect our relationship with God. Thankfully, we recalibrate and adjust our direction as we learn from Scripture. Paul told the Colossians, "Since, then, you have been raised with Christ, set your hearts on things above, where Christ is, seated at the right hand of God. Set your minds on things above, not on earthly things."[22]

Jesus understood that we're concerned with our basic needs, like food or clothing. But He reminds us to "seek first his kingdom and his righteousness, and all these things will be given to you as well."[23] When we trust God's provision, we can release worry and focus our time, thoughts, and energy on God's purpose for us.

---

20   Proverbs 21:2
21   1 Peter 3:4
22   Colossians 3:1-2
23   Matthew 6:33

In Paul's second letter to Timothy, Paul used the example of household items to help explain that the transformation of our inner selves prepares us to serve God. He contrasts gold and silver items used for special tasks to those made of wood and clay that were intended for everyday use.[24] When God makes us holy, we become like the special tools, ready to be part of His plans. When we put aside distractions, we can instead look for righteousness, faith, love, and peace. These are sacred qualities that God looks for in a human heart.

Solomon penned multiple proverbs about seeking the Lord's wisdom. As we turn the pages of Scripture, we discover God's priorities. We learn what love is; how to love our neighbors and enemies; and, most importantly, to love God with every ounce of our heart, mind, soul, and strength. When we get off track and begin to go through the motions of ritual or religious habits, Micah's prophecy sets us straight by reminding us to "act justly and to love mercy and to walk humbly with your God."[25] If we start to look at outward actions and appearances, we can return to God's Word to redirect our heart towards Him.

Seeking God with our whole hearts is an incredible challenge in this world full of difficulty and pain. It certainly couldn't have been easy for Eliab to navigate feelings of rejection after being passed over by the Lord in favor of his youngest shepherd brother. Additionally, this devastation occurred in sight of his community, no doubt producing shame. These feelings are understandable, real, and valid. Challenges and suffering hurt us; and it's unrealistic to think that we must ignore our emotions, as if pretending they aren't there is a mark of spiritual maturity. God sees our pain. He's near to the brokenhearted. However, we're not meant to hold on to the hard emotions that entangle our hearts. God is with us, and He wants to heal us.

Eliab was acutely jealous of David. As we know, jealousy grows and spins off hatred like a furious hurricane, preventing us from loving God and our neighbor. Paul addressed this issue in the Corinthian church, pointing out

---

24   2 Timothy 2:20-21
25   Micah 6:8

the envy and quarreling among them, calling it worldly. When we cast aside our tendency to look at earthly things and set our hearts on seeking God, we discover that it requires His love to overcome coveting. Paul reminded the Corinthians that "love does not envy . . . [or] boast" but instead is patient and kind.[26] Additionally, Proverbs 10:12 tells us that "love covers all wrongs." When our hearts are full of holy compassion, there's no room for jealousy or hate.

But the wounds from Eliab's rejection followed him to battle against the Philistines, spurring an angry response when David visited the Israelite camp. Bitterness has a habit of establishing itself within us, becoming a fixture in our hearts that's increasingly difficult to remove the longer it dwells there. Just as love pushes out jealousy, bitterness pushes out joy and peace. It clouds our vision so we can't see God's blessing or recognize His presence. Though He never leaves us, we become unaware of Him and feel isolated from our Heavenly Father, missing out on much of His goodness.

If Eliab hadn't made peace with David, the consequences could have been dire for either of them. Had he remained in Saul's army, there might have been division between the tribe of Judah under his lead and Israel with David as king. Similarly, our tight grasp on bitterness has excruciating results in our relationships and daily lives. Paul urged, "If it is possible . . . live at peace with everyone."[27] Even our enemies should be treated with kindness as we "overcome evil with good."[28] He says, "Get rid of all bitterness, rage and anger, brawling and slander, along with every form of malice. Be kind and compassionate to one another, forgiving each other, just as in Christ God forgave you."[29] When we replace bitterness with God's kindheartedness, we fully experience love in community as well as in our personal relationship with Him.

The root of Eliab's jealousy was likely disappointment. He expected to achieve greatness, probably based on his position and experience as the oldest

---

26   1 Corinthians 13:4
27   Romans 12:18
28   Romans 12:21
29   Ephesians 4:31-32

son. How often do the seeds of disappointment sprout pain in us? When we feel we deserve something better or our expectations are shattered, we experience devastation. Extreme sadness is natural when this happens, but allowing it to take up residence in our hearts is an obstacle to healing. It's easy to develop nearsightedness and only see the immediate loss of a dream or frustration when things aren't going well. Stepping back into God's perspective expands our vision and gives us hope.

We must remember that the story isn't over. Eliab's journey didn't end on the day that Samuel anointed David, and our journey doesn't abruptly end with our disappointment. God promises that He'll complete the work that He started in us. Meanwhile, while we plan our course, God directs our steps. We aren't in this alone; we aren't solely responsible for life's outcomes. Staying close to the Lord and discerning His vision not only gives us direction, but it also encourages our spirits.

The prophet Jeremiah compared one who trusts in God to a tree planted by water. Our security in God gives us confidence like the tree who has roots by a stream. It's not afraid when heat or drought come, and its leaves are always green and full of fruit.[30] We can allow God to establish our expectations, even when things aren't going well. This might mean patiently spending more time in prayer before rushing into a big decision or perhaps accepting challenging situations while seeking understanding. Like a healthy, well-rooted tree, we won't be swayed by disappointment, bitterness, or jealousy.

We mustn't forget that our identity is firmly established in Christ, Who shields us from shame and humiliation. Eliab had to face the elders and community after his rejection. It would've been easy to doubt everything about himself after being passed over by God. When we experience shame, we forget our identity and worth. Questions and self-doubt uproot our security in the Lord. But when we take our eyes off the outward appearance of a humiliating situation, we can instead remember that God created us and knows

---

30 Jeremiah 17:7-8

us intimately. We were adopted as children through salvation in Jesus and are securely surrounded by the everlasting love of God. This is immovable and unchanging. We can confidently declare, "For I am convinced that neither death nor life, neither angels nor demons, neither the present nor the future, nor any powers, neither height nor depth, nor anything else in all creation, will be able to separate us from the love of God that is in Christ Jesus our Lord."[31] Assurance of our relationship with God puts embarrassment and shame into perspective. He is our Refuge, healing our hearts as we reach out to Him in our pain.

What was God's purpose for Eliab, and how do we see His plans for us in our own bleak circumstances? Being a king wasn't the only role to fill; God had plans for Eliab from the day he was born. His leadership skills had a place in the army, with his family, and with the tribe of Judah. Even as king, David couldn't possibly do everything alone. A trusted, capable brother by his side would have been a great support. Eliab was a crucial piece in God's intentions for Israel, a smaller but necessary part of the big picture.

As we've seen before, God values each of us without the rankings that people assign to one another. God designed and treasured Eliab. Little is recorded about him, but we can imagine how he eventually blessed those around him, in his close relationships and within his community. He wasn't the king, but he had a vital role. Just as each day of Eliab's life mattered, ours do, too. Every time we talk to a neighbor, are part of a team, or pray for someone, we are walking in God's purpose for us and playing a significant role in His kingdom. Meanwhile, our impact extends beyond what we can see. Eliab probably couldn't imagine that the story of someone rejected and cast aside would be part of God's great narrative told for centuries. His heart's transformation from jealous anger to brotherly peace reaches from history into our thoughts today. He is remembered as we read his story; and most importantly, Eliab is remembered by the God Who knows our hearts.

---

31   Romans 8:38-39

CHAPTER 7
Gehazi

Based on 2 Kings 4-5 and 8

The soothing breeze on Mount Carmel lifted Gehazi's spirits with each deep breath. It was quiet today; the rustle of tree leaves and a chorus of bird songs kept him company. Frequent travels with his master, Elisha, had left him weary. Wherever the prophet and his servant went, something always happened, whether an act of God or the clamor of people seeking Elisha's attention. After the exhaustion of road life, Gehazi was always eager to return to the peace of Mount Carmel. Though holy days here were always bustling, the rest of the time was much calmer.

The steady rhythm of his everyday tasks allowed him to daydream and reflect on recent events. But his deep thoughts were brought to a sudden halt when Elisha's voice caught his attention.

"Someone is coming!" The prophet directed Gehazi's gaze down the mountainside. Squinting, the servant saw a woman and a man on donkeys in the distance, heading their way.

"That's the Shunammite woman, but why would she come all this way on an ordinary day?" Elisha wondered. "Hurry to her. Find out if something's wrong with her husband or son."

As Gehazi scurried down the hill, he puzzled over what could require the hours-long trek from Shunem other than the Sabbath or special holy days.

The woman was quite wealthy, so surely she could've sent a messenger. A personal visit must be driven by a matter of great importance.

She had extended generous kindness to Elisha and Gehazi. The two were always welcomed with a warm meal whenever they passed through Shunem. One day, she surprised them with a prepared room where they could stay each time they were in the city, giving them more security when they traveled. After long days on dusty paths listening to Elisha deliver God's messages, Gehazi was grateful for the rest and hospitality.

Elisha, too, was thankful. On a visit a few years ago, he asked Gehazi, "In what way could God bless her?"

The servant thought for a moment. "Her husband has lived many years, but they don't have any sons. Maybe . . . "

Immediately, Elisha summoned the woman. He promised, "In a year's time, you'll be caring for your baby boy."

She protested, "Please, don't let me hope for such a thing!"

Although that seemed to be the end of the conversation, she did indeed give birth to a son the following year. During each visit with the Shunammite family, Elisha and Gehazi watched as the child grew from a toddler to an energetic young boy. He was clearly the light of the woman's life and a joy to everyone in their home.

But now, as Gehazi reached the woman and her servant, he noticed that the boy wasn't with her. Before he could ask, the woman reassured him, "Everything's fine." However, she didn't pause for even a moment and kept the donkey moving steadily toward Elisha. Gehazi trailed behind, trying to keep up with the pace of the animals.

She arrived ahead of a breathless Gehazi, then jumped off her donkey and flung herself at Elisha's feet. Gehazi knew how tired his master was after constantly dealing with people. This was his time to rest, and he needed space! Gehazi rushed to pull the woman from the ground before Elisha but was abruptly halted by the prophet.

"Let her be!" Elisha scolded. "She's in great distress, but the Lord hasn't revealed to me the reason." Then to the woman, he asked, "What's wrong?"

"I didn't ask you for a child! Didn't I tell you not to make such a promise? Yet at your word, God gave me a precious boy, whom I love so deeply. And now, He's taken Him from me." The woman couldn't continue through her tearful sobs.

Quietly, Elisha turned to Gehazi. "Secure your cloak, and go as quickly as you can with my staff. Don't stop to talk to anyone. When you get there, place the staff over her son's face."

Dutifully, Gehazi grabbed the wooden staff and prepared once again to sprint down the mountain. He knew Elisha and the Shunammite woman would be close behind him, but every minute was crucial—this was an emergency. The memory of the laughing boy danced in Gehazi's mind, motivating him to keep a steady pace over the next sixteen miles. He had seen many miracles happen through Elisha; this time, it was his turn to be used by God!

Gehazi's legs trembled as he finally arrived at the house in Shunem. He didn't pause to greet the servants but rushed up to the familiar room where he had stayed so many times. He found the pale body of the boy, cold and unmoving on the bed. It unnerved Gehazi for a moment to see the once-spirited child so lifeless. But this wasn't the end. He knew what to do. Quickly, Gehazi laid the staff on the boy's face as Elisha instructed. He stepped back and watched for the Shunammite son to sit up with new breath, but he did not stir.

Maybe it will take a minute, Gehazi thought.

But time seemed frozen as the boy's eyes didn't flutter open nor did his chest rise and fall with air. The servant expected to hear a cry as he woke, but there was silence. It was no use. The child was truly gone.

Gehazi dreaded returning to his master and the Shunammite woman with the devastating news, but perhaps it was best that they knew before they arrived home. He hurried to meet them on the road and quietly told them, "I'm so sorry. I don't know why, but the boy didn't wake up."

Elisha didn't say a word but neither did he slow his stride toward the upper room. Leaving the woman to be consoled by her family, Gehazi followed Elisha to the bed where the deceased son lay. Surely, Elisha would grieve. The prophet was fond of the boy, cherishing years of friendship with the family. This would break his heart. Gehazi stepped toward Elisha, who shook his head and closed the door, leaving the servant outside.

Stunned, Gehazi stood and stared at the door as questions flooded his thoughts. *Did his master need a moment alone to mourn? Was he crushed by the failed miracle? Why didn't the staff awaken the boy? Where was the power of God? Was it because Elisha was special and Gehazi was not?*

Shadows crept into the house as the sun dipped behind the mountains. He heard Elisha's footsteps in the upper room, and the muffled sound of his voice was followed by periods of silence. Gehazi was certain that the prophet was praying; and he paced in front of the closed door, uncertain of what to do without clear instructions. It was quiet again, and then . . . *Was that a sneeze?*

The door flung open, and Elisha urgently told Gehazi to bring the Shunammite woman. In a heartbeat, she raced up the stairs, followed by Gehazi. As he reached the upper room, he saw the woman get up from Elisha's feet and then embrace her living, breathing son. With tears streaming down her cheeks, she put her hands on her son's shoulders, looked into his eyes, let out a cry of thanks, and then led him downstairs to the rest of the family.

The prophet's work continued. As time passed, Gehazi witnessed more miracles, including the transformation of poisoned stew into a safe dinner, as well as a crowd of a hundred men fed by only twenty loaves of bread. The hand of God worked through his master each day. But as exciting as the miracles were, Gehazi was always grateful for quiet respites in Elisha's home. Today was such a day, until a neighbor told Elisha about the king.

He said that the king received an alarming letter from the ruler of nearby Aram, who was sending the commander of his army to Israel to be cured of leprosy. Israel's king knew he could not possibly heal disease; and fearing the start of a fight, he tore his robes and cried out in despair. So Elisha sent a message suggesting that the king should direct the sick commander to him.

A few days later, the commander arrived at Elisha's house accompanied by an entourage with horses and chariots. Elisha sent Gehazi out with instructions.

The servant told the commander, "Go to the Jordan River and bathe yourself in its water seven times. You will be made well; your skin will be healed; and you'll be clean once more."

The hope in the commander's eyes clouded, and his face reddened with anger. "What is this nonsense? Where is the man of God?" He turned away from Gehazi and led his entourage away from the prophet's house. Gehazi watched as they left, shrugged his shoulders, and returned to his work.

He was slightly shocked when, a couple of days later, he heard approaching hoof beats and the squeak of chariot wheels. The commander had returned; but this time, he was visibly healthy! Gehazi called Elisha, who met the Aramean at the door.

The commander, full of gratitude, spoke to Elisha. "I know now that Israel's God is the only God anywhere."

He offered Elisha a generous gift of thanks, but the prophet refused. The commander then requested some dirt from Israel so that he could build an altar to the Lord once he returned to Aram. With the soil and Elisha's blessing, he began the journey back home.

But Gehazi could not get the offer of extravagant gifts out of his mind. *Why shouldn't we enjoy blessings after doing the Lord's work?*

Filled with determination, he slipped out of the house and ran after the commander. It wasn't long before he saw the chariots in the distance, moving at a casual pace. Soon, he nearly caught up with them and caught the commander's attention.

"Is something wrong?" asked the concerned Aramean.

"Everything is fine," Gehazi answered as he approached. "My master sent me to tell you that some young men of the prophets have just arrived. Can you give them some silver and a couple sets of clothes?"

The commander was more than happy to provide the gifts and gave Gehazi twice the amount of silver he requested. Once Gehazi returned home, he put the silver and clothing away, then returned to serve Elisha.

"Where were you, Gehazi?"

Quickly, he answered, "I have been here."

But Elisha would not tolerate lies. "I know that you met the commander! Do we now accept money, goods, or other gifts? Now the commander's leprosy will be forever upon you and your descendants!"

Elisha closed the door, and Gehazi had to walk away from his life of service to the prophet. One glance at his arm confirmed the prophet's words to be true. As his skin became white, Gehazi knew that the consequences of disobedience were much greater than the treasures he once desired.

The people had survived seven years of famine by the time Gehazi found himself speaking to the king. The ruler requested information about Elisha, and Gehazi was more than happy to testify to the great things he had witnessed while he served. As he regaled them with the account of the Shunammite woman and her son's new life, he was surprised to see her walk in with the boy to see the king as well.

She explained how she had lost her house and land after following Elisha's instructions to wait out the drought in the land of the Philistines. Then she humbly requested that it be returned to them.

"My king, this is the woman, as well as her son that Elisha brought back from death!" Gehazi exclaimed.

Since the king could barely believe the miracle was true, he asked the woman for more details. She enthusiastically told him about the wonder of her son's birth, his sickness and death, and the incredible healing that had brought him back to life. The king was amazed and declared everything that belonged to her before the famine should be returned, including the profit earned from her land since she had left it. Once again, Gehazi saw God provide for the faithful Shunammite woman who extended great kindness to His prophet.

• •

By now, we've seen that not all of our sidelines stories feature role models; but even difficult narratives provide insight for us. In this case, we're mostly learning from Gehazi's mistakes, not his example. In the end, he was self-serving, opportunistic, and greedy. How did Elisha's chosen right hand man stray so far?

Gehazi demonstrates the struggle between serving God and serving ourselves. The tension between self and service can last a lifetime. Just as the folks in the pages of Scripture grappled with these issues, so do we as we make one choice at a time between the Lord and selfish ambition. In Galatians, Paul contrasts gratifying the desires of the flesh with walking in the Spirit. He describes human sins—such as immorality, discord, and hatred—then reminds us that the Holy Spirit produces love, joy, peace, and other gifts.[32] Serving ourselves brings harm, while abiding in the Lord yields blessings.

In His Sermon on the Mount, Jesus taught that we cannot serve two masters and therefore it's not possible to "serve both God and money."[33] Wealth itself is merely an object; but the love of it, full of greed and self-interest, can rule over us if we allow it. Pursuing power is another way to serve ourselves. So are seemingly small daily choices we make in our own favor at the expense of others or with disregard to the Lord. However it manifests in our individual lives, the bottom line is that we can't serve both God and self.

What does serving God look like in practicality? Jesus also said, "Whoever serves me must follow me; and where I am, my servant also will be. My Father

---

32   Galatians 5:16-25
33   Matthew 6:24

will honor the one who serves me."[34] Following the footsteps of Christ will lead us directly into His service. In addition to prioritizing our time and resources for His glory and kingdom work, it also involves caring for our neighbors. After Jesus' parables in Matthew 25, He described separating those who served Him from those who neglected Him. He rewarded those who gave Him food, drink, clothing, shelter, and care when He was in need. But the people responded in confusion. They didn't remember ever encountering Jesus in need and helping Him. But He explained that whenever they were compassionate to brothers and sisters in need, they were also loving the Lord.[35]

Let's return to Gehazi's story, long before Jesus taught His disciples. It was always unmistakable that following God meant caring for His people. Gehazi probably knew this from a young age, as well as from watching Elisha demonstrate God's principles. It's no surprise that Gehazi cared for the Shunammite woman when the prophet asked how they could express gratitude for her hospitality. Gehazi thoughtfully pointed out that she was childless, subtly suggesting that might be a way to bless her. He had a special position in proximity to Elisha; and from that place, he advocated for someone else's need.

When we find ourselves on the sidelines, we are often specially positioned to be an advocate for someone in need. We know what it's like to receive this support, as the Holy Spirit is an advocate for us, coming to our aid when we struggle. Jesus described the Spirit as a Helper; and Paul said in Romans, "The Spirit helps us in our weakness. We do not know what we ought to pray for, but the Spirit himself intercedes for us through wordless groans. And he who searches our hearts knows the mind of the Spirit, because the Spirit intercedes for God's people in accordance with the will of God."[36]

Similarly, the Lord instructs us to advocate for our neighbors. In Proverbs 31:8-9, words attributed to King Lemuel share wisdom he received from his mother: "Speak up for those who cannot speak for themselves, for the rights of

---

34   John 12:26
35   Matthew 25:31-46
36   Romans 8:26-27

all who are destitute. Speak up and judge fairly; defend the rights of the poor and needy." This echoes lines from the psalmist Asaph, who wrote, "Defend the weak and the fatherless; uphold the cause of the poor and the oppressed. Rescue the weak and the needy; deliver them from the hand of the wicked."[37] Throughout Scripture, God tells us to stand up for those who are struggling and to amplify the voices of the unheard. Justice is important to Him as He cares for us, and we are called to serve Him by advocating for others.

Unfortunately, Gehazi appeared to lose compassion for the Shunammite woman years later when she rushed to Mount Carmel in distress. Instead of supporting her as she fell to Elisha's feet, Gehazi attempted to put a barrier between the upset woman and the prophet. What shifted in Gehazi? Was this a case of misunderstanding? Was he so focused on serving Elisha that he thought he was doing the right thing? Without more information, we can only speculate; but it's our first red flag that Gehazi was headed for trouble. Thankfully, he demonstrated faithful obedience when he ran to help heal the Shunammite son. When he was in the king's presence, he promoted Elisha and indirectly helped the Shunammite woman. But by the time he met Naaman, the commander from Aram, Gehazi had turned his devotion from God's holy work to his own desires.

This is a good time to note that theologians are unsure of Gehazi's timeline and question if 2 Kings was written in chronological order. If Gehazi met with the king after he had been given leprosy, there are quite a few uncertainties. It was unlikely that a king would have close contact with a leper, which suggests that the incident occurred before Gehazi's illness or that his health was restored at some point. We lack the necessary information to know his motivation or the circumstances that led to meeting the king. This complicates our examination of Gehazi's journey from faithful servant to a foolishly selfish leper, but the sad reality remains: he let himself be pulled in the wrong direction.

---

37 Psalm 82:3-4

The interesting thing about being on the sidelines is that it can be deceptive. While we mistakenly think that we aren't being noticed, we're actually in a place of significant influence. Gehazi had the ability to help the Shunammite woman and the responsibility to represent Elisha (and the God of Israel) to the Arameans. We, too, have the opportunity to support others or make trouble through our choices. Our actions and the resulting consequences of our decisions affect others as well as ourselves. Will we decide to be an uplifting advocate? How are we representing the Lord in our daily interactions? Whom are we serving? Will we help or hurt? We must frequently ask ourselves these questions or risk straying like Gehazi.

When we look up from the story and think about what happened beyond the text, we might wonder how Gehazi's actions affected the Shunammite woman and her son in the long term. We could question Elisha's experience with a loyal servant who became a hindrance. What was it like for him to lose his assistant after so many years together? Seeing the story through Naaman's eyes inspires us to ask how his story ended. Did he faithfully serve God in his homeland? Was his understanding of the God of Israel changed after his encounter with Gehazi? What did he tell family and friends when he returned to Aram with a mound of dirt and plans to build an altar?

We can also ask how the king was changed when Gehazi told him about God's miracles through Elisha. Gehazi may have been a servant, but he had influence and a farther reach than he realized. We can't be fooled into believing the lie that we have less value during difficult seasons full of trials. We may not see the complete effects, but the results of our obedience to God (or disobedience) rarely end with us.

In fact, sometimes our place on the sidelines provides an extraordinary view. Imagine watching a theatrical performance from the wings instead of the front row. The close-up look reveals details that can't be seen from the audience. Gehazi had more than a front-row seat to God's wonders through Elisha. He was even occasionally invited to participate! Yet, somehow,

Gehazi missed it. The miracles didn't resonate within him, leaving a lasting impression. He wasn't changed from the inside out; and he didn't love God with his entire heart, soul, mind, and strength.[38] Gehazi walked away from Elisha's ministry and a proximity to the amazing things God was doing right before his eyes.

Gehazi was ordinary, and his experience was more common than we might have initially realized. Whether we're in the spotlight or backstage, we have the opportunity to zoom in on God's work. Sometimes, He seems to do more incredible things in the lives of people around us. Instead of feeling left out, we might understand that we've been invited to witness His beautiful miracles; and often, we get the opportunity to participate. Once again, we have choices. Will we pay attention and see what He's doing, or will we be distracted and miss it? How will we contribute—as a help or as an obstacle? Can we celebrate and praise the Lord for His hand in the details or will we mope in the shadows without considering His bigger plan?

It can be discouraging to feel like we're missing God. There can be many reasons for this; but in Gehazi's case, it's because he wasn't looking in the right direction. If our eyes are set on something other than the Lord, it can be extremely difficult to see Him in our peripheral vision. So many things clamor for our attention: worry, comparison and envy, anger, difficult circumstances, and yes, selfishness. This isn't a complete list, but it's more than enough to pull our gaze from Christ. But when these obscure our view, we must focus our vision on Him to block out all the earthly distractions. David sang, "I keep my eyes always on the Lord. With him at my right hand, I will not be shaken."[39] Jesus explained that our hearts are with what we treasure, so we must choose to value eternal heavenly things instead of temporary material goods.[40] We will move toward the object of our focus, so it matters where we set our eyes.

---

38   Mark 12:30
39   Psalm 16:8
40   Matthew 6:21

Gehazi almost got it right. He was so close to knowing God well, but he chose the path that led away from His goodness. He missed riches of blessings greater than any of Naaman's gifts because he didn't realize that the Lord and His true treasures were in closer proximity to his heart. Gehazi's story invites us to examine our own hearts and evaluate our choices. May we take the path that follows and serves Christ, leading to His abundant life.

CHAPTER 8
Huldah

Based on 2 Kings 22–23 and 2 Chronicles 34

Activity bustled around Huldah the prophet as she strolled through the temple courtyard. Years of disrepair were finally being addressed at the command of King Josiah; and with every step, she was encouraged to see carpenters, builders, and masons restore the sacred building to its former beauty. The workers seemed in good spirits as their chatter mingled with the clamor of tools. Perhaps yesterday's discovery inspired their work today.

Huldah's husband, Shallum, had been eager to share the news when he returned from the palace last night. As the keeper of the wardrobe, he was often near royal activity. In the sixteen years since young Josiah took the throne, both Huldah and Shallum had witnessed incredible changes in Judah. People were uncertain about an eight-year-old child in the highest authority; but with the guidance of his wise advisors, King Josiah had grown into a young man who loved the Lord and followed His ways. Some said that he reminded them of his ancestor, the great King David. His reign was certainly quite a change from the reigns of his father and grandfather, who were motivated by evil. Judah had become a nation of idol worship, straying from the God Who cared for them since the days of Abraham, Isaac, and Jacob.

After years of working to remove high places and idols from Judah, King Josiah now shifted his focus to temple repair. While supervising the renovations, the high priest, Hilkiah, uncovered something exciting. Shallum recounted the details to Huldah over their evening meal.

"They were examining part of the foundation when Hilkiah started shouting! It was the Book of the Law! We've only heard about it all these years, and now to actually see it in person is incredible," he said, nearly breathless with wonder. "Then he gave it to Shaphan so he can include it in tomorrow's report to the king."

Shallum's enthusiasm sparked optimism in Huldah. She frequently prophesied in the temple, and her advice was often sought by the king and royal officials. But she wanted to be certain not to miss anything today. Perhaps that was why she walked a little more deliberately, listening a little more closely than usual. Suddenly, loud voices filled the courtyard. Huldah saw Hilkiah making quick strides past the workers, heading toward her. He was accompanied by Shaphan the scribe and three other attendants. They began speaking before they even reached the prophet.

"Huldah! The king sent us to seek the Lord," Shaphan began. "After I reviewed the Book of the Law yesterday, I brought it to him. When I read some of it aloud, he was greatly distressed."

"He cried out and tore his robes in grief," continued Hilkiah. "Then he sent us to you for a word from the Lord. King Josiah, on behalf of all of Judah, wants to know more about the Law. He acknowledged the Lord's anger against us because of the disobedience of our ancestors."

The courtyard was now silent, so Huldah and the men stepped into a secluded corner for privacy. After a moment of thought, the prophet spoke.

"The Lord of Israel says to tell the king, 'I will send disaster here and over the people, just as you have read. Because the people have turned away from me, worshiped other gods, and incited my anger by their idolatry, my rage will be like flames against this place and will not be extinguished.'"

All five men stared wide-eyed at Huldah, taking in every word.

"Tell King Josiah, 'This is what the LORD God of Israel, says: Because you were moved and sincerely humbled yourself before Me when you heard my words—that the people would be made desolate—and because expressed your grief and cried out to me, I listened to you. Therefore, after you have died, you will be laid to rest peacefully. You will not witness the catastrophe I will bring here.'"

Hilkiah nodded solemnly. The prophecy was complete, and the king urgently needed to hear it. The men thanked Huldah for her faithful service, then made their way back to the throne.

The next few weeks were a whirlwind. Once King Josiah heard the words of the Lord, he summoned all the people of Judah to hear the Book of the Law for themselves. Huldah joined the gathering in the crowded temple. When the king stood by a prominent pillar, every conversation ceased and every eye was on their trusted ruler. He read the sacred words and once again agreed to their covenant with God, promising that the people of Judah would break the evil patterns of previous generations. They pledged to follow God's commands with everything they were and all that they had. Huldah could barely hold back tears as she watched them return to the Lord. She knew how much Josiah loved God, and to see his devotion passed on to the people filled her with joy.

True to his word, King Josiah leaped into action. He took any item made for a false god out of the temple and burned it. He removed priests who worshiped idols from their positions and destroyed every remaining trace of disobedience to God's covenant. From Jerusalem and throughout Judah, the king obliterated idols, altars, and remnants of false worship. When this work was finished, King Josiah once again issued an order to all the people. They would resume celebrating the Passover as described in the Book of the Law.

Huldah knew that every word of the Lord's prophecy would happen as He said. For now, she was grateful for the faithfulness of their good king and this short period of peace. She once again stepped into the restored temple courtyard, ready to give more of God's messages to His people.

●●●●●●●●●●●●●●●●●●●●●●●●●●●●●●●●

Huldah is often quickly forgotten when we recount the exciting story of King Josiah's sweeping reforms. We marvel at the dramatic discovery of the Book of the Law, which was likely parchment or scrolls that scholars believe could have been what is now Deuteronomy. Huldah's somber prophecy moves the action forward, but then we're easily caught up in Josiah's quick and thorough response as he rallies the people of Judah. Their commitment to the Lord is in stark contrast to many generations of idolatry, and the king's destruction of all false worship was extreme but necessary. That is what captures our attention, and the role of the humble prophet fades into the background.

Just as Josiah and Hilkiah responded to the words of the Lord with respect and urgency, we, too, have something to learn from Huldah's message. God "is the same yesterday and today and forever."[41] Therefore, we can trust that His words endure through the centuries. From this particular prophecy, we learn that God keeps His Word and that obedience is how we love Him.

It's possible that Josiah read these words from the Book of the Law: "Know therefore that the LORD your God is God; he is the faithful God, keeping his covenant of love to a thousand generations of those who love him and keep his commandments."[42] Scripture and history are full of examples of God's great promise-keeping. We see how He kept His covenants with Noah, Abraham, and the nation of Israel. The more we study the Word, the more we see how it holds true today. We can watch as He follows through on assurances to care, protect, and provide for us. Difficulties may last painfully long, and the care may not appear the way we expect; but we can trust that He'll continue to love us. We can hold on to the hope of eternity and Christ's return. God told Huldah and Josiah that though there would be a short period of peace, His

41   Hebrews 13:8
42   Deuteronomy 7:9

people would still experience the consequences of their sin. That's exactly what happened, demonstrating once again that the Word of the Lord is true.

The prophecy was not only about punishment but also shone a light on the path to blessing. God's love and grace are gifts that He gives freely. While straying from the Lord leads to destruction, the outcome of obedience is full of His goodness because His commands help us fully experience life. Josiah found peace as he followed God's law, and we'll discover the same and more as we do likewise. Additionally, obedience is one of the ways we worship. The apostle John explained, "This is how we know that we love the children of God: by loving God and carrying out his commands. In fact, this is love for God: to keep his commands."[43] Worship is more than attending a church service or singing a hymn. Our obedience also demonstrates love, respect, devotion, and adoration to the Lord. Actions show that our words are sincere, and keeping God's commands truly expresses sincere worship.

A closer examination of Huldah's story reveals principles that go beyond the words of her prophecy. She also demonstrates the importance of speaking truth from the sidelines, even when it's difficult. Though we don't walk through ancient temples or serve in royal courts as she did, the struggle to tell the truth in all circumstances is timeless. We might choose small fibs to spare someone's feelings, blatant lies to avoid trouble, or convoluted stories to maintain some kind of control over challenging situations. Despite the temptation to take what seems to be the easiest approach, only truth pleases God. He wants us to be honest and trust Him to handle the results. It's unmistakable that His love rejoices in the truth.

In the fifteenth Psalm, David wrote, "The one whose walk is blameless, who does what is righteous, who speaks the truth from their heart . . . Whoever does these things will never be shaken."[44] When we find ourselves on the sidelines, we might not realize how much our honesty matters. We

---

43 1 John 5:2-3
44 Psalm 15:2, 5

forget that it affects other people and can change outcomes. As we've learned, God can use us in mighty ways when we're not the center of attention; so it would be a mistake to think that it doesn't matter what we say or do. Speaking truth is crucial to honoring God and loving those around us. In Ephesians, Paul pointed out that we must avoid falsehood and speak truthfully to our neighbor in order to live in unity.[45] God commands us to love one another, and genuine love demands complete honesty.

Paul also gave guidance to his son in the faith, Timothy. He said, "Do your best to present yourself to God as one approved, a worker who does not need to be ashamed and who correctly handles the word of truth."[46] Serving the Lord when we feel like we're behind the scenes requires obediently telling the truth, especially during difficulty. Huldah's prophecy was not entirely good news for the people because God's anger would not be easy to endure. But it was necessary for them to know the severity of the situation, understand the vital need to turn to obedience, and trust that God would carry out what He said He would do. After all, if He was consistent with discipline, He would also be faithful to keep the covenant of love He vowed never to break. The hope of restoration could overcome their fear of punishment.

Many of our previous sidelines examples taught us that the size of our role is not the true measure of importance. Though King Josiah held the highest human power in the land, he still needed Huldah's help. Her obedience led to the public reading of God's law, the renewed covenant, and massive reforms throughout Judah. More thorough research of Scripture shows that two well-known prophets, Jeremiah and Zephaniah, were both actively prophesying at this time. However, God chose Huldah to deliver this crucial message. While it was not uncommon for women to be prophets in the ancient Near East, the biblical text only highlights a few, such as Miriam, Deborah, and Anna. Huldah's story is found in a few mere paragraphs, but it's strikingly significant.

---

45   Ephesians 4:25
46   2 Timothy 2:15

Though her prophecy was brief before she quickly exited the story, we easily see how crucial she was to the entire nation of Israel.

Jesus told His followers a parable that demonstrated that simple beginnings can lead to greater participation in God's kingdom. In the story, a man gave three of his servants varying amounts of money to keep while he went on a trip. Two of them used the funds in a way that increased the amount, while the third put his away for safekeeping. When the master returned, he praised the first two, saying, "'Well done, good and faithful servant! You have been faithful with a few things; I will put you in charge of many things.'"[47] The third servant, however, was reprimanded for not managing the money better.[48]

While this simple story helps us understand that small things have great value, there was a real-life boy whose seemingly meager offering became more than he could dream. Jesus had been teaching a large crowd of over five thousand men, plus women and children. As the day wore on, the people became hungry but were far from any source of food. One boy had packed a lunch of two fish and five loaves of bread; and he generously offered it to Jesus, who multiplied it into enough to feed all the people.[49] One kid, who probably didn't feel the least bit special, was a key part of blessing an entire community. His story has been recorded and told for generations, and his example of obedient generosity is a model for our giving today. Our human obsession with the size or superiority of tasks is not how God measures success. Jesus explained to His followers, "'Are not five sparrows sold for two pennies? Yet not one of them is forgotten by God. Indeed, the very hairs of your head are all numbered. Don't be afraid; you are worth more than many sparrows.'"[50] Details matter to the God Who cares for sparrows and counts hairs.

Let's return to Huldah. Though many of the prophets were well-known and had an extremely public presence, Huldah's ministry appears to be

---

47   Matthew 25:21, 23
48   Matthew 25:14-30
49   John 6:1-14
50   Luke 12:6-7

limited to Jerusalem. She's an excellent reminder that renown is not the goal. Public adoration is a hollow reward, and we can't allow lack of recognition to keep us from serving and fulfilling our God-given purpose. Huldah isn't mentioned anywhere in Scripture outside of the similar accounts in 2 Kings and 2 Chronicles. Though we have only a small amount of information about her, we can safely assume that she was respected for her prophetic gift. King Josiah and Hilkiah entrusted her with the vital task of authenticating the Book of the Law. This probably wasn't the first time Huldah spoke God's Word to the king, and it would've taken many prophecies to build Josiah's confidence in her. She consistently served the Lord for many years before being part of a turning point for Judah. Without such humble dedication, she may not have been called upon by the king at all.

Instead of popularity, our aim is to seek humility. James put it simply when he wrote, "Humble yourselves before the Lord, and he will lift you up."[51] It's not our job to point the spotlight at ourselves. In fact, when we try, the results are dismal. We often end up looking disingenuous or foolish. Proverbs 11:2 points out that "when pride comes, then comes disgrace, but with humility comes wisdom." When we're busy honoring ourselves, we have little capacity to honor God. That's dangerous territory to enter—a slippery slope that can start to look like false worship. We saw that happen when the people of Judah ventured down a similar path.

Humility is another way to love our neighbors. Paul instructed believers not to think more highly of ourselves than we should but instead use judgment along with the faith God has given us. This doesn't mean we need to lower our self-worth, but we need to understand that we're God's dearly loved children and we're cherished just as much as each of our brothers and sisters. He continued by bringing attention to community, describing our unique differences as parts of the same body of Christ. Our gifts might include prophecy, serving, teaching, encouragement, generosity, leadership,

---

51   James 4:10

or mercy; but none of these are superior to the others. They're all used to love our neighbors and strengthen one another.[52]

Humility allows us to live peacefully together; but pride puts us above others, causing division and strife. When we view ourselves and others as God does, we find it easy to prioritize our neighbors more than our own interests. We can serve and give wholeheartedly, extending the care that God so graciously lavishes upon us. This puts more value on others' well-being, which helps our communities thrive. Without humility, our ability to love our neighbor is considerably hindered. So to overcome pride, we look to God's guidance. Keeping His laws helps us remain humble, step by step. This includes gratitude, confession, service, and intentional time in His presence.

Huldah's faithful service was a treasure to King Josiah. All the people of Judah were blessed by her wisdom and dedication to the Lord. Though she never received the notoriety of other prophets in her day, she had a tremendous impact on history. She proved trustworthy and ready to be called upon in a high-pressure situation. Without her on the sidelines, the nation would have lacked crucial direction. Huldah's steady presence connected them to the God of covenants and helped them return to their compassionate Lord.

---

52 Romans 12:3-8

CHAPTER 9
Sons of Hassenaah

Based on Nehemiah 2:17–13:31

Every ear listened intently as Nehemiah's voice rang out with confident authority. The large crowd knew he had held a high position in the Persian king's court, but he also shared their Jewish ancestry. Both his heritage and power brought him back to their home in Jerusalem, though it was merely a shadow of what it had once been. The people now lived among ruins with faint memories preserved only by their grandparents' stories, recollections passed down from their own fathers and mothers.

Hassenaah's sons stood among Jerusalem's men as Nehemiah continued. Their family had returned from exile a few generations ago, and they only knew this version of the city—crumbling, surrounded by foreign neighbors, and still subject to distant Persia. At least, the temple had been repaired a few decades ago. Now, the possibility of new restoration inspired hope in the brothers.

"Jerusalem is in extreme disrepair; not even the gates were spared from fire," said Nehemiah. "But together, we can reconstruct the wall and put an end to our shame."

He explained how God guided him from royal service to his arrival in Judah and that He listened to Nehemiah's prayers. God made a way for Nehemiah and granted him favor with the king, who gave his blessing for Nehemiah to leave his post and travel back to Judah. With trust in their leader, Jerusalem's men were eager to begin this ambitious project. Nehemiah described their approach: they would divide into teams, each focused on a specific section of the wall. They were ready for their assignments.

The sons of Hassenaah were in charge of the Fish Gate, previously one of the main entrances to the temple and closest to the fish market. They gathered their tools without delay to secure wooden beams in place and attach doors, bolts, and bars. It was important to stay in communication with the men working nearby—Zakkur on one side and Meremoth on the other— to maintain consistency throughout the wall. This was how they heard the news about enemy opposition.

Nearby foreign officials were unhappy with Jerusalem's new construction project. Immediately, they mocked Nehemiah and his builders, accusing them of rebellion against the king. They knew Israel's history and were intimidated by the possibility of strength and unity among the Jews. Surely the Persians would never allow a potential uprising! They couldn't let the Israelites regain independence! But Nehemiah was unshaken, responding only with the assurance that the Lord would make them successful.

Hassenaah's sons worked diligently, repairing the wall alongside Jerusalem's men and even some women. They progressed quickly, drenched in sweat from the hot sun. Day after day, the city was surrounded with the sounds of tools and the shouts of the determined builders. But rumors of danger were passed along the wall from worker to worker; and just as construction reached the halfway point, a new threat emerged. The angry foreign officials, led by a leader named Sanballat, advanced from their usual taunting ridicule to form actual fighting plans. Neighboring groups united against the Israelites, ready to strike. The sons of Hassenaah grew weary as they pressed on with construction, and everyone around the wall was tired and overwhelmed by the constant work removing the never-ending rubble. Discouragement set in, and the people grew disheartened.

"Our enemies are getting closer. No matter what we do, we can't stop their attack!"

Their fearful whispers became loud exclamations as the Israelites' fright increased, and guards were posted all day and through the night. But Nehemiah did not relent. They would repair the wall, and no one could stop God's plans. Encouraged by their faithful leader, the sons of Hassenaah refused to give up. They were committed to their goal and continued to rebuild the Fish Gate. The workers employed a new strategy: half of the men continued to build; and the other half traded their hand tools for spears and bows, positioning themselves to defend Jerusalem from an enemy assault. If they carried materials, they worked with one hand and held a weapon in the other. Even designated builders wore swords at their sides. Their muscles were tense and their ears alert for any sound of approaching trouble, allowing any sudden movement to easily startle them. With divided attention, they checked the quality of their work while simultaneously assessing their safety.

They took Nehemiah's words to heart: "Don't be scared. Remember our powerful and astounding Lord, then defend your people and our dwellings."

This approach seemed to work. The wall was nearly finished, with only the completion of doors and gates remaining. The sons of Hassenaah, though exhausted, pushed through to make sure that the Fish Gate was ready and at its best. They heard reports of Sanballat's attempt to lure Nehemiah into a trap, but God gave their leader wisdom and safety. And then, after fifty-two days of hard labor and perseverance, the men finally put down their weapons and tools, stood back, and beheld the completed wall.

Soon after, the sons of Hassenaah joined the rest of the Israelites near the Water Gate. Ezra, Judah's trusted teacher, read from the Book of the Law that the Lord gave Moses long ago. When Ezra opened the book, everyone stood; and when he praised God, all the people shouted agreement as they bowed to the ground in worship. The Levites helped explain the reading to the Israelites, which brought the people to mournful tears as they understood its meaning and recognized how sinful they had been.

Suddenly, Nehemiah stepped up. "This is a holy day! Don't cry sorrowfully; but instead, eat and drink in celebration! Share with those who aren't ready. Again, this day is special and dedicated to our Lord. Don't mourn because the Lord's joy fills you with strength!"

The atmosphere became one of rejoicing in Jerusalem and throughout Judah. The sons of Hassenaah marveled at the Law that was now much clearer. They listened each time Ezra read more of God's Words and put them into practice. From celebrating a festival with temporary shelters made of branches to a solemn confession of sins, the Israelites served the Lord and followed His instructions.

The day came to dedicate the wall. It had taken every ounce of their ability, bravery, and persistence; but it was worth the dangerous trouble. Hassenaah's sons once again joined their community as music echoed through the city, replacing the sounds of construction that had filled their streets for nearly two months. The leaders of Judah stood on top of the wall while two choirs voiced songs of gratitude. People offered sacrifices to the Lord as everyone, young and old, rejoiced so loudly that the noise could be heard far beyond Jerusalem's new, strong, secure wall.

• •

The sons of Hassenaah are a bit of a mystery. The text doesn't tell us how many brothers there were, their ages, their names, their skills and occupations, or individual identities. They're acknowledged only as a group, with no other details beyond their designated wall segment. We aren't even sure if Hassenaah was their literal father or if they were descendants of Senaah, whose people returned to Judah from exile nearly a hundred years before Nehemiah arrived to restore Jerusalem's wall.

But Scripture tells us everything we need to know about the sons. Their personal details are trivial compared to their dedicated service. They were responsible for constructing the Fish Gate, working well with their neighbors, and responding to outside intimidation. Without their contribution, the wall would not have been completed as planned. Additionally, these men have something to teach us about our own place on the sidelines. Unconcerned about personal credit and recognizing the importance of teamwork, Hassenaah's sons generously gave their time, effort, and skill. Their example shows us that success is not always measured by individual achievement; but instead, we honor God when we put aside self-importance to be united for the good of our community.

No matter how we feel on the sidelines, we're never alone and certainly never unnecessary. We're not merely warming a bench while everyone else is in the game. When we're a selfless part of a team, we're indispensable. Our participation is vital! When a situation is not about us, we might think that we have no reason to stick around. Yet in God's plan, everyone has a distinct role. A beautiful blend of individuals that forms a cohesive group produces results we could never achieve on our own.

Nehemiah's wall-builders were recorded and preserved in history. This tells us that their contribution was notable and most certainly crucial. It took everyone to complete such a massive project, especially so quickly and while under enemy threat. Every section of the wall needed to be strong for it to be effective; a gap or weak segment could bring another disaster upon Jerusalem. Every single worker mattered.

Cooperation is needed in the body of Christ today. We've already learned that we all have something to contribute, equipped by our unique design to fulfill part of God's purpose. This was demonstrated in the early church as the believers came together. Paul wrote, "So Christ himself gave the apostles, the prophets, the evangelists, the pastors and teachers, to equip his people for works of service, so that the body of Christ may be built up."[53] Our skills aren't only for self-enrichment or personal gain. It takes everyone's participation for our churches, families, communities, and perhaps even our world to be complete.

---

53 Ephesians 4:11-12

When we evaluate God's plan for our lives, we often look only at our situation. We ask, "Where do I belong? What should I do? What do you want for me, Lord?" However, His purpose for our lives extends far beyond our own reach. To live life abundantly involves the entire family of God. We can ask new questions, such as "What are the needs in our community? How can my abilities contribute to solutions and improvements? What do you want for us, Lord?"

In his letter to the Ephesians, Paul once again used his illustration of the human body to remind them that the family of Christ is joined together as if by "every supporting ligament."[54] Each part does its work so that we can grow in love. If our physical body had a missing or injured ligament, we would experience discomfort, pain, or immobility. There are few parts of our bodies that we can function without. Imagine what would be missing if we withheld anything that we have to offer. This principle is so important that Scripture repeatedly emphasizes the significance of teamwork and unity.

Sometimes, our tasks might surprise us. Jerusalem's wall-builders included priests, district rulers, women, and craftsmen like goldsmiths and perfume-makers to help repair the wall. Our willingness to step out of our comfort zones allows God to do mighty things through us. What could we accomplish with the Lord if we set aside our fears and tried something new? Like Peter stepping out of the boat to walk with Christ on rolling waves, we might be surprised at what we can do when we ignore perceived human limitations and look only to the Lord. The risk is worth it because it can also benefit our community. Doing something beyond our typical habits can produce life-changing results that benefit many others.

In case we need more convincing that we aren't meant to do everything ourselves, we can read the wisdom of Solomon: "Two are better than one, because they have a good return for their labor: If either of them falls down, one can help the other up."[55] The Philippian church learned about this

---

54   Ephesians 4:16
55   Ecclesiastes 4:9-10

togetherness with Paul's support. Our ability to connect with other humans is made possible by our relationship with Jesus as we try to be like Him.

> Therefore if you have any encouragement from being united with Christ, if any comfort from his love, if any common sharing in the Spirit, if any tenderness and compassion, then make my joy complete by being like-minded, having the same love, being one in spirit and of one mind. Do nothing out of selfish ambition or vain conceit. Rather, in humility value others above yourselves, not looking to your own interests but each of you to the interests of the others. In your relationships with one another, have the same mindset as Christ Jesus.[56]

Paul continued his letter to describe Christ's humility, reminding us that even though Christ is one with God, He didn't use that to His advantage as He served in love. This led to His death on a cross that was typically associated with shame; but His sacrificial love redeemed, rescued, and reconciled humanity. God exalts Christ, and He ultimately receives the greatest glory.[57] When we aim to be like Jesus, we also put down our self-focused ambition in favor of sacrificial love for our brothers and sisters. We look for God's wide-reaching plans and can understand our humble place in them while seeing others through His perspective.

When we let go of our ego, the good of the community becomes the priority. We're like a tiny piece in an intricate mosaic, and the masterpiece would be incomplete without our small part. There isn't much glory in our little piece alone, but beauty emerges in togetherness.

Paul also encouraged believers by offering his own life as an example. While he served in ministry, he didn't seek wealth or material things. He worked to provide for his own needs and to support other people who traveled and served with him. Paul understood that he had a limited role to play as the gospel spread in all directions, reaching Jews as well as Gentiles. Through Paul's

56   Philippians 2:1-5
57   Philippians 2:6-11

ministry, God transformed hearts, changed lives, and established new church communities. Paul was only one ordinary person out of many who taught and supported new believers, accepting abuse, injury, and even the threat of death. Though we might be less familiar with other early church leaders, they were also part of a much larger picture, enduring suffering so that the body of Christ would flourish. Paul urged the church to follow his lead and sacrificially care for others; and as modern-day disciples, we're also motivated by this teaching.

Following Christ includes pursuing His priorities, rooted in—but not limited to—love, justice, peace, and truth. Jesus told His disciples, "Whoever wants to be my disciple must deny themselves and take up their cross daily and follow me. For whoever wants to save their life will lose it, but whoever loses their life for me will save it."[58] The cross was an instrument of death; and right before this statement, Jesus told His followers that He would be killed. This wouldn't have happened if He hadn't allowed it because human ability can't thwart God's power. Instead, Jesus chose the cross in exchange for our salvation.

Of course, there are many ways for us to lay down our lives besides physical death. Whenever we trade our desires for the benefit of others, we put aside our own interests. When we do this to follow Christ, He replaces our limited concerns with eternal matters, guiding us into a life vastly more fulfilling than anything we could imagine. We lose our mediocre version of life, and He saves our souls. Our nearsighted look at our world is replaced with the vision of His much bigger and more amazing plan.

The sons of Hassenaah also showed us that God can transform human struggles into His goodness and glory. Jerusalem's wall was a massive construction project. It required intense effort, manual labor in the heat of the day, cooperation with a great number of people spread out over a significant distance, and heavy oppression from enemies. Being part of this extreme challenge required perseverance and dependence on the Lord. It was tempting to quit when enemy threats overwhelmed them and the scope of the project

---

58   Luke 9:23-24

seemed impossible. The completion of the wall was only accomplished by the power of God; the people required His strength and protection to achieve their goal. When it was finished, it was clear to everyone, including the surrounding nations, that Israel's God was great and that His hand was on His people. They built more than a protective barrier around the city. Through this project, the Israelites established a testament to the Lord's incredible omnipotence.

God transforms our challenges, too. In 1 Peter, we read about the hope we receive from Christ's mercy, assuring us that our suffering is temporary and won't last forever. Like gold, we are refined through trouble; we grow as we learn and draw closer to Christ. But our faith is of far greater value than gold, and we will live eternally with Christ.[59] And while refined gold might shine, the glory of God is exceedingly brighter, shining for the world to see the great love of our Almighty Creator. Our difficult journeys display God's nurturing involvement in our lives, showcasing His never-ending abilities and presence in the lives of His children.

Paul explained, "We also glory in our sufferings, because we know that suffering produces perseverance; perseverance, character; and character, hope. And hope does not put us to shame, because God's love has been poured out into our hearts through the Holy Spirit, who has been given to us."[60] God doesn't bestow pain upon us to teach us a lesson or punish us, but He does transform the hardship and give it purpose (whether it's a result of sin or if, like Job, we happen to find ourselves in tangled up in difficulty). Isaiah 61:3 describes God giving us a crown of beauty instead of ashes, joy in place of mourning, and praise for despair. The Lord works "all things" together "for the good of those who love Him, who have been called according to his purpose," explains Paul in Romans 8:28. Our labor for Him is never in vain.

We should also note that it doesn't mean that the only way to truly serve God is through suffering. Often, we experience delight as we obediently

---

59   1 Peter 1:6-7
60   Romans 5:3-5

follow Him. After all, He's a loving God Who gives us joy, peace, love, goodness, and more gifts through His Spirit. But such a powerful, Sovereign, and compassionate Father can create blessings out of painful experiences as well. When Paul wrote, "I can do all this through him who gives me strength" in Philippians 4:13, he was describing being content in every situation, whether in need or with plenty. Just as God's glory is displayed through His blessings, we also testify to His greatness when we walk with Him through trials.

So we have great hope that God will change our suffering into something glorious for Him. God brought light out of darkness, and He also shines in our hearts. We are given His power instead of our own. We might be hard-pressed, perplexed, persecuted, or struck down; but we are not crushed, in despair, abandoned, or destroyed.[61] The One Who raised Jesus from the dead also gives us life. So we can persist through difficulty, knowing that "our light and momentary troubles are achieving for us an eternal glory that far outweighs them all. So we fix our eyes not on what is seen, but on what is unseen, since what is seen is temporary, but what is unseen is eternal."[62]

If we believe that our seasons on the sidelines are useless, we might try to patiently endure them until something more exciting happens or the focus shifts back to us again. But if we do this, we'll pass by God's incredible blessings in teamwork, unity, and His compassion for us all. We would withhold our gifts when others desperately need them. We could miss a magnificent display of His glory while wallowing in self-pity instead of rejoicing with our neighbors. Putting ourselves aside and stepping readily into community is an act of kindheartedness. As we are filled with the love of Christ, we can follow His example of selfless service, devoting ourselves to the greater good.

---

61   2 Corinthians 4:8-9
62   2 Corinthians 4:17-18

CHAPTER 10
Job's Wife

Based on the Book of Job

Life was extremely good. It was nice to be married to a wealthy man who was sometimes celebrated among all those who lived in the East. He was a wonderful husband and father; but more importantly, he was righteous and followed God. His name was Job, and his wife delighted in the comfortable security of their family while their ten grown children, seven sons and three daughters, lived happily nearby. The fertile region of Uz was filled with their livestock; and many servants managed thousands of sheep, camels, oxen, and donkeys. Even more were busy helping Job's wife tend the homestead.

Their quiet life was filled with extravagant joy. Their children also loved to celebrate special days together with feasts and merriment. Job remained watchful over his sons and daughters, offering sacrifices after their parties and making sure they were in good standing before God, just to be certain that any overlooked sin was covered. His wife was proud of them all and felt especially honored to be married to this man.

Years of comfort left Job's wife unprepared for the disaster. It began like every other day as she managed the servants from the cool of their tents, sheltered from the desert sun. The kids were feasting once again, this time hosted by their oldest son. Perhaps she and Job would visit later and bring more wine in case they ran out before their celebration ended. She was about to ask her husband if he would like to see them, too, when a messenger shouted for Job as he ran toward their tent. This was the moment that would destroy her life forever.

"Sir, I have horrible news!" he began while trying to catch his breath. "While we were tending the oxen and donkeys, enemies attacked us and plundered them all. And, sir, I'm so sorry, but they killed everyone; I'm the only one who escaped."

They couldn't quite grasp this loss before another distressed messenger approached.

"Master, something terrible has happened! Fire from Heaven burned up all your sheep along with the servants. I'm the only one who made it out alive!"

Job's wife realized that this was a catastrophic hit to their wealth and security, but she knew that they could handle it with Job's reliance on God's provision and wisdom. She never expected a third messenger to appear in the next moment.

"I'm so sorry, Job," he said with tears forming in his eyes. "There were raiders who overtook us, stealing the camels and killing each servant with swords. I was the only one who managed to get away to tell you."

Job was speechless. His wife knew that the possession of their herds established their prominence, but that was worthless compared to the human lives they lost on this terrible day. Heaviness flooded their home when a fourth messenger rushed into the homestead so distraught that they could barely understand his words. Job's wife felt her heart nearly stop as her world shattered when he spoke.

"Your sons . . . Your daughters . . . They were enjoying the feast when a sudden, powerful desertgale blew in . . . The house . . . All four corners were struck. It collapsed. I'm so sorry. All of them . . . have died."

She heard the shrieking wail before she realized it came from her own soul. Job's wife collapsed to her hands and knees, tears darkening the dirt beneath her. Job's own anguish joined her pain. Time seemed to stop until, suddenly, he got up. After ripping his robes in great sorrow, he shaved his head as a sign of mourning. But what he did next was beyond his wife's comprehension. Job worshiped God.

"The Lord gave everything to us and now the Lord took it all away; yet I still praise His name," he nearly whispered through his despair. Even in the darkest of days, Job remained righteous.

The days passed in a blur, as if they were moving through a silent, dense fog. The few remaining servants tended to Job and his wife, each carrying their own burden of great sadness. If they had to speak, they hushed their voices to preserve the quiet. Suddenly, the stillness was pierced by Job's scream. His wife ran to his side, trying to understand what had overcome him. His body was healthy only this morning but now was covered in dreadful sores from his scalp all the way down to the tips of his toes. Servants quickly attempted every remedy they knew in hopes of alleviating his suffering. Nothing could ease the fiery lesions, leaving Job's wife standing by helplessly. Would her husband join her children in death? She could not bear to lose the man who anchored her world. Her love for Job was not enough to save him and watching him writhe in pain was more than she could stand. She looked away, so at least he wouldn't see her uncontrollable weeping.

Job no longer entered their tent. Perhaps he wanted to prevent anyone else from sharing his disease, but it was his intense mourning that kept him in a pile of ashes. He was nearly unrecognizable with his bald head and skin ravaged from scraping shards of pottery over his oozing sores. He refused to eat, no matter how many times his wife sent servants to his side. She wondered if his physical pain was equal to the agony in her heart. She barely knew how to function from minute to minute. If she was fortunate enough to briefly drift to sleep, nightmares plunged her deeper into the darkness.

There was no relief for either husband or wife. That day of tragedy was only the beginning of their never-ending misery.

Today, she wouldn't send a servant. Instead, she ventured to Job's bed of ashes herself. Over the past few days, her tears had dried and turned into anger. Even through her husband's suffering, how could he abandon her? He wasn't the only one who had lost it all. They were her precious children, too. And what good was his worship of God? Why hadn't the Lord saved her sons and daughters? Why didn't He see Job's faithfulness and prevent the house from falling at all? None of it was just; none of it made sense. But if Job intended to spend his remaining days wasting away in the dirt, he would leave her as a stranded widow. She might as well die, too.

A pungent, rotting odor intensified with each step toward her husband's well-worn place among the ashes. She stopped at the edge, not able to bring herself to touch the soot and dirt. Her own grieving could barely be contained, but she lacked the energy and ability to express the kind of mournful display that Job had chosen. It took everything she had just to survive each day. She should be speaking to her daughters today, hearing their latest news and all about their brothers' escapades. Instead, she stared at what was left of Job as he finished praying. He then became silent, and she could no longer hold onto her words.

"Are you still stubbornly holding on to religious principles?" she nearly spat. "Just renounce God, then give up! Why live?"

Job's eyes were filled with both pity and defiance. "You are speaking foolishly." He was right; this wasn't her typical demeanor. The heartbreak had changed her. Job continued, "Should we only accept God's good gifts but not difficulties?"

Everything Job's wife thought she would say abruptly fled her mind. She couldn't argue with a man who remained devoted to a cruel God, despite all that He took away. Her husband was clearly beyond reason. Without a word, she turned her back on him and retreated to her home, where the shadows would shield her from the world. She couldn't understand how it continued to exist, anyway.

She saw Job's friends before they reached his ashes. Eliphaz, Bildad, and Zophar had been loyal to Job for many years. Perhaps they could soothe him as she could not. Maybe they would even convince him to leave the dirt and allow a servant to tend to his festering wounds. Job's wife watched from a distance as they stepped closer to Job, bending low to meet his eyes. She heard their own cries, as they wept alongside her husband.

In disbelief, she saw the three men tear their own robes, scoop ashes from Job's pile, and sprinkle it on their heads. Then they sat. Gradually, they grew quieter until only the occasional rustle of leaves and grass in the wind interrupted the silence. And for seven days and seven nights, the loyal friends remained at Job's side without speaking a word, offering only their comfort.

The next few months produced an awkward routine. After their week of intense quiet, Eliphaz, Bildad, and Zophar begin to speak with Job.

Good, thought Job's wife. *Perhaps they can reason with him now that some time has passed.*

She kept her distance, occasionally sending servants to the men with food or water. Sometimes, she would venture down to the ashes herself so that she could extend personal hospitality to their friends. She overheard their passionate discussion, at times almost scolding Job and accusing him of responsibility for their calamity. Job's wife felt vindicated and frequently agreed with them. But Job made some compelling points, as well. She wasn't sure if her heart was softening toward the man she loved or was merely growing dull as grief evolved over time.

Eventually, a fourth friend joined them, a young man named Elihu. He apparently had much to say but was so soft-spoken that Job's wife didn't know if he was blessing or cursing her husband. She would have to let God sort it out. He was going to do what He wanted, anyway, and she was powerless to change His mind.

Then one day, the dry desert heat gave way to a humid breeze. As the day went on, it became a chilly wind, ushering in ominous, towering clouds. Job's wife and the servants ran for cover as a storm unlike anything they had ever seen brightened the sky with lightning. Thunder rolled and crashed without ceasing, and Job's wife realized that her husband and his friends remained in the ash pit. She huddled in her safe, dry tent, shuddering with each clap of thunder. This storm was the most powerful she had experienced, and even the air felt alive. Suddenly, the rain ceased. The air was still, and the oppressive gray clouds slowly cleared to reveal blue sky. But what astounded Job's wife most was that her husband stood—for the first time in months! He looked up to the sky and spoke loudly. She crept closer to hear his words.

"Lord, I have heard Your voice! I know that You are almighty, and nothing can stand in the way of Your reasons and plans." There was a new humility in his voice, different from the self-pity since the disaster. "I said things I didn't comprehend. They were beyond my understanding. You said that You would ask the questions, not me. Though I had knew of You, now I've truly seen You; and so I humble seek forgiveness in this dirty ash pit."

Something about Job's tone calmed the bitterness within his wife. She wasn't yet ready to let go of her resentment toward the Lord, but maybe it would be better if Job returned to her side. Her heart felt a spark of hope when Job took a few slow steps to leave the ashes. His friends spoke together and left with a promise to return immediately. As Job walked toward his wife, she thought perhaps his sores didn't look as grotesque as they had been. It had been so long since she felt any light in her life that she had forgotten what it was like. Now that the storm was clearing, could there be sunny days ahead?

Recovery from their trauma was slow but steady. Job's wife accepted that the place within her that deeply loved her children would always ache, but it would not destroy her. She witnessed Eliphaz, Bildad, and Zophar offer burnt sacrifices to God, accompanied by Job's prayers. Job was healed; and once the news spread among their friends and family, they were eager to see him after months of being too afraid to visit. Their generous gifts helped Job and his wife restore the riches they had lost, and she considered the idea that the God Who had let her down might be providing for their family after all. Through shared meals and consoling words, their community comforted the couple.

Job and his wife began to rebuild their lives, starting with obtaining livestock again. The animals numbered twice the size of their previous herds, and soon, Job's wealth doubled, too. His wife watched his faithful worship of God and listened as he explained that God's tender justice prevailed over their heartache. She wasn't quite sure she understood it completely, but Job's loving example encouraged her to trust the Lord. With each passing year, their family grew; and they were blessed with ten more children. The laughter of seven sons and three daughters filled their home once more, amplifying the love they shared. Life would never be the same as it was before the disaster, but it was good. With God's hand upon them, it was again extremely good.

●●●●●●●●●●●●●●●●●●●●●●●●●●●●●●●

Sometimes, life becomes so difficult that we feel like we're being punished without reason. We watch from the sidelines as friends and family seem to handle everything with ease while we struggle to hold on. Challenging circumstances accumulate before we finish taking care of the most recent trial, and we wonder how much more we can take before we break. In these seasons, we can surely cry out to God. But what will we say to Him, and how will we say it?

Job's wife's story is one of profound grief. As we turn each page of the biblical book, we get a close-up of Job's journey, thoughts, and actions. We see "behind the scenes" to the spiritual realm, which helps us contemplate some of the purpose found in suffering. God makes it clear that Job didn't earn his pain because of anything he did. Instead, God, Who created and maintains the universe, is just, with reasons beyond our comprehension for what happens to us. As modern readers, we can find meaning in Job's story that includes giving God glory and worship in the hardest times. But what about his wife? Why was she whisked along for the terrible whirlwind of a ride? Why was she required to endure such intense loss and grief? Was God at her side, too?

If the Bible recorded every detail, it would contain more volumes than we could count. However, we can look at God's consistent character to help us understand what might not be evident on the page. We know that God is unchanging and that He treasures every person; therefore, God treasured Job's wife and never left her. Her life had meaning like Job's, even if she wasn't featured on much of history's stage. But she could not see God's cosmic perspective, and she lacked her husband's level of faith. The trauma of losing everything—and possibly fearing that she could lose Job to his disease as well—left Job's wife angry and resentful toward Almighty God.

From tragedy and great loss come grief and anguish. Job worshiped God and called out to Him with questions; but his wife took the opposite course, cursing God and suggesting that they give up. Job's wife gives us the opportunity to assess our response to adversity. How do we approach God during disaster? What is our reaction when we don't feel we deserve the trials that plague us? Once again, during our study of the sidelines, we can learn from a person's mistakes. First, we can see that God doesn't abandon us, no matter how desperate a situation might be. Whether we are experiencing the consequences of our choices or suffer by no fault of our own, God is perpetually near, not only beside us but going ahead to prepare a way as well. Then, we can understand that not only is the Lord present, but He also truly sees our pain.

We're learning that though the world may not recognize or notice us, God knows us intimately. He understands our turmoil and doesn't ignore our anger and despair. We're never left behind to fend for ourselves; instead, our loving Heavenly Father attentively cares for us. A look at the Psalms shows us that David understood this, too. After God saved him from an enemy pursuit, he penned these words: "The righteous cry out, and the LORD hears them; he delivers them from all their troubles. The LORD is close to the brokenhearted and saves those who are crushed in spirit."[63] Another psalmist echoed the theme, singing, "He heals the brokenhearted and binds up their wounds. He determines the number of the stars and calls them each by name."[64] Our God, who gives each star in every galaxy an individual name, is even more compassionate toward each human on earth. And lest we believe that He is watching our struggle from afar, He assures us that He's right in the midst of it with us, healing and tending to our hurts.

Remembering this truth is vital when we don't see or feel the Lord. Job's wife could only see the catastrophe. Her children were gone, and her husband was barely surviving in a pit. It likely seemed as though God had abandoned her, too. She must have had as many questions as Job did, if not more. But instead of seeking answers, she dispensed hurtful words. Many have criticized Job's wife as merely being another of Job's tormentors. But she was also a real person, experiencing tragedy and vulnerabilities. She shows us that we have great influence in desperate situations, even when we feel helpless. From the sidelines, we unfortunately have the ability to bring ourselves and others down as if we were a destructive force. It's crucial to be aware of this and remember that the opposite is also true: we can encourage and carry God's light into the darkness instead. Offering a kind word, a loving gesture, or a whispered prayer amid despair is a powerful way to uplift a friend.

Many Scriptures remind us that the tongue holds great power. Our words don't disappear into the air as they leave our mouths but can transform situations in both positive and negative ways. They extend beyond our own experience and affect others. Jesus explained that our words originate in our

---

63 Psalm 34:17-18
64 Psalm 147:3-4

hearts, and Job's wife demonstrated what happens when a bitter heart speaks. Proverbs 12:18 likens reckless speech to piercing swords but advises that wise words bring healing. Job's wife could have been a supportive presence; but lost in her own pain, she added to the couple's suffering. If our speech is a symptom of what's truly going on inside, then we must be attentive to our hearts.

In the apostle James' letter, he wrote that "everyone should be quick to listen, slow to speak and slow to become angry."[65] Job's wife's rage overtook much of the love within her, resulting in excruciating contempt. When we're hit with adversity, we need the love of God to survive. Often, we, too, become consumed by hurt and anger, turning on our loved ones as we lose control of our circumstances. Just as Job's wife didn't know why she and Job experienced extreme calamity, we also find ourselves losing sight of the source of adversity that is truly against us. Instead of addressing the root of our problems, we lash out at the people around us. Paul explained that "our struggle is not against flesh and blood, but against the rulers, against the authorities, against the powers of this dark world and against the spiritual forces of evil in the heavenly realms."[66] God was not Job's wife's enemy. What if she had united with Job in seeking God? How could she have changed the narrative for herself and her husband? When we're on the sidelines, we're in an essential position. If we prepare now to stay connected with the Lord when disaster strikes, we will be driven by His love and wisdom during a crisis.

Despite the darkness that surrounded her, light finally returned to Job's wife. God restores things that are lost; this is part of His character. Though Scripture doesn't mention Job's wife in the epilogue, it also doesn't say that God gave Job a new spouse. Therefore, we can assume that he was married to the same woman throughout the story and that she was part of the Lord's restoration.

Their family's healing brings hope to us all. God returned wealth to Job and his wife, and He can do the same for us after seasons of great loss. In

---

65   James 1:19
66   Ephesians 6:12

His restoration, He takes great care to reestablish more important things beyond material gifts, such as relationships, peace, or our joy. While their lost children could never be replaced, God's gift of ten more was an abundant blessing to the couple. Today, He promises to provide care for each of our souls and can be trusted to come through after seasons of loss. First Peter 5:10 declares, "The God of all grace, who called you to his eternal glory in Christ, after you have suffered a little while, will himself restore you and make you strong, firm and steadfast." We don't know how long that "little while" might be, which often intensifies our struggle. Perhaps that's why Scripture doesn't tell us the exact timeline of Job's story. God knows our tendency to compare ourselves with our neighbors, and He wants us to rely on His perfect timing as He carries us through.

At times, we need internal healing and repair. Though the story doesn't give us a description of Job's wife's repentance and reconciliation, it also doesn't tell us that she remained a hindrance to Job for the rest of his long life. We can only guess at the details; but since we know God's tender care for His children, it's likely that He rehabilitated her heart as well. Even when our bitterness takes over, we aren't beyond His forgiveness. One of King David's greatest sins was adultery, and he was moved to repentance after the prophet, Nathan, confronted him. In Psalm 51, David confessed and asked the Lord for forgiveness, requesting a clean heart, joyful salvation, and a willing spirit. Of course, the Lord did just that; and David is still remembered as a man who deeply loved Him.

Although at times we walk in dark valleys, we never need to navigate difficult paths without God. Furthermore, we are merely passing through; the valley is not the end. Restoration is our destination as God gives us everything we need and more. As the shepherd-turned-king, David described the greatest Shepherd in Psalm 23. He pointed out that we can confidently rely on the Lord to restore our souls as He leads us on righteous paths for the sake of His name.

Job's wife endured a season of great trouble, and she did not handle it well. However, her response didn't prevent God's powerful grace. It might be easy to dismiss her story after her defiant outburst, but that's not where it ended. It's not the finale to our story, either. Our night of suffering may last longer than we think we can bear, but God will not leave us there. He hears our cries, sees our pain, and compassionately nurtures us through it. He fills us with His love so that we can navigate the storm, encouraging others who are also struggling. He promises that we're never abandoned, and He'll always provide everything we need. This gives us hope, along with assurance that the sun will indeed shine again.

CHAPTER 11
The Rooftop Friend

Based on Matthew 9:2-8, Mark 2:1-12, and Luke 5:17-39

He's back! The news spread quickly through Capernaum, faster than a sudden afternoon storm on the Sea of Galilee. Jesus had returned to their waterside town after visiting nearby villages, healing the sick, and telling anyone who would listen about the kingdom of God. He often stayed with Peter, a local fisherman and friend; and the neighbors said that today He would speak at Peter's house. A crowd was gathering quickly; but if they hurried, they could hear what Jesus had to say. Perhaps they would even see a miracle!

One young man was eager to meet the person who many said was God's Son. Residents of Capernaum scurried down the street toward Peter's home, and this young man jumped to his feet to follow. The house wasn't far away; he could get there before the crowd grew too large. But the idea lingered for only a moment, and then he looked down at his friend reclined on the floor. His friend couldn't race to see Jesus with the rest of the community. He was occasionally left behind, since his legs wouldn't carry him at any speed and his paralysis often left him discouraged.

However, the support he received from his buddies lifted his spirits. The standing young man paused for a moment. How could he see Jesus without leaving his disabled friend behind? Suddenly, three more of their excited companions appeared. They had all heard that Jesus healed Peter's mother-in-law the last time he was here, and they didn't want to miss anything He might do today! That's when inspiration struck.

The young man knew this was their chance. If Jesus healed so many people in the surrounding region, why not heal their friend here? There wasn't much time. Quickly, the four abled young men gathered around their friend's mat, each securing a corner. Yes, this might work! They had carried him before and could move in step with one another. Carefully, they rushed to Peter's house with the rest of the neighborhood.

They didn't need to walk far, but it appeared that they hadn't arrived soon enough. People swarmed around the courtyard outside the house, obscuring the door as they clamored to see what was happening inside. The young men recognized many neighbors, but some strangers were there, too; they looked like teachers of the law and Pharisees. Every few seconds, someone would try to hush the crowd's impatient chatter so that they could hear the Teacher speak. It would be impossible for even one of the young men to get in, so they might as well give up on the idea that all five of them could see Jesus. Maybe if they had known sooner that Jesus was here, they could have made it in time. Perhaps they would have another opportunity on a different day to bring their friend to the Healer. Today, the paralyzed man was not alone in his disappointment.

At that moment, something caught the abled young man's eye. Someone had left a coil of rope next to an adjacent house. He looked back at Peter's home, past the crowd at the door, and to the stairs leading up to the roof. What if they still had a chance to see Jesus?

Immediately, the four friends formed a plan. If they were fast and didn't draw attention to themselves, they could get to the top without anyone noticing. The roof tiles were sturdy enough to support their weight but easy enough to remove. It was a bold idea, but their friend was worth it. They knew that Jesus could heal him, changing his life completely once he was able to walk.

They acted as one and carried their paralyzed friend up to the roof. After he was gently placed to the side, they began to hastily remove the tiles beneath their feet. Though they worked as quietly as possible, it wasn't long before people inside noticed pieces of hardened mud falling on their heads and light filling the room. The young men remained focused, carefully opening a hole large enough for their friend and his mat to fit through. They could talk to Peter about roof repair later. Right now, the most important thing was to get the paralyzed man to Jesus.

A hush enveloped the crowd as Jesus stopped speaking and looked up at the sunlight filtering through swirling dust. The young man met His eye and saw only kindness. Encouraged, he reached for the rope, and the four friends secured the paralyzed friend to his mat. This was the riskiest part because one mistake could cause serious injury. Slowly, the young men lowered their friend through the ceiling and into the center of the house, right in front of Jesus.

Jesus looked at the men above Him and then turned His attention to the paralyzed friend. "Son, your sins are forgiven."[67]

Every person in and out of the house was silent. The young man watched intently from above, waiting for the miracle to appear. How would it happen? Would his paralyzed friend feel strength fill him at once or gradually? How intense would it be? Why wasn't he standing up? Jesus wasn't saying anything else, even though the crowd waited expectantly. This wasn't how His previous healings had gone.

From the roof, the young man's heart sank. No doctor had been able to heal his friend, and this was their last desperate hope. Abruptly, Jesus turned to some of the teachers of the law.

He asked, "Why do you think that?"

What did He mean? The man on the roof was confused. No one had said anything but Jesus.

---

67   Mark 2:5

The Teacher continued, "Which is easier: to say to this paralyzed man, 'Your sins are forgiven,' or to say, 'Get up, take your mat and walk'? But I want you to know that the Son of Man has authority on earth to forgive sins."[68]

Jesus looked at their paralyzed friend, and the men on the roof held their breath in anticipation.

"Stand, return home, and make sure to take your mat with you."

As Jesus spoke, the young man saw his friend's eyes widen. Obediently, the previously paralyzed friend stood confidently and grinned at Jesus, Who smiled at him in return. The healed friend rolled up his mat and began to make his way through all the people and out the door. His four buddies scrambled off the roof and down the stairs to meet him.

With great joy, he shouted, "Praise God!" and all five young men nearly skipped down the familiar streets of Capernaum. Their hearts were so full of wonder and celebration that they barely heard all the people at Peter's house exclaiming their own praises, marveling that they'd never seen anything like this. The young man watched as his friend practically danced through town to begin a new season of life, thanks to the Lord.

●●●●●●●●●●●●●●●●●●●●●●●●●●●●●●●

These are the kind of friends you'd want to have, and they're a vibrant example of the potential of the sidelines. Despite being told in three Gospels, this story reveals little about the people involved. In fact, some details, such as the possibility that the miracle took place at the home of the disciple Peter, have been suggested by scholars after extensive research. We can only speculate about the lives of these five men before and after the Divine healing.

But what we do know for certain is beautiful. We know that this paralyzed man was not abandoned to a solitary life due to his disability but was supported by a loyal group of friends. They were willing to do anything necessary to help because they all believed that Jesus had the power to heal. The four friends displayed generous compassion without expecting

---

68   Mark 2:10

to gain anything more than rejoicing with their companion. Dedication, perseverance, and an abundance of love transformed their seemingly ordinary place on the sidelines into something so extraordinary that it echoes through the ages.

We find that our rooftop friend was motivated, focused on a goal, and not discouraged by a crowd or obstacles. It appears that the Lord gave him the gifts of creativity, resourcefulness, and problem-solving. This friend did not stop pursuing Christ, despite difficult circumstances. We applaud his efforts as we also remember that God equips us to handle any situation that comes our way. Not only did the friend show great personal character, but he also demonstrated the goodness of the Lord.

God did something similar during the days of Moses. When the Israelites left slavery in Egypt, they were pursued by Pharaoh's army. Just as they thought they reached a dead end at the edge of the sea, Moses told them, "The Lord will fight for you; you need only to be still."[69] Then God parted the water and led them to safety. This is the same God Who handles the hurdles in our path, which gives us the confidence we need to keep running our race. Since every person and situation are unique, God doesn't do everything the same way. We might see a miraculous wave-parting solution, or He might show us each single step as we participate in His work. But consistently, our Almighty God is present and active, helping us and always in control, and continuously making a way for us. We can bring our faith in God's help to the sidelines, persisting when those around us are struggling.

The rooftop friend persevered. Perhaps it was his faith that encouraged him not to give up, or maybe it was his devotion to the paralyzed man. Whatever his motivation, he shows us that enduring through trials is yet another way we can be blessings from the sidelines. We encourage others by our words as well as our actions. An Old Testament example of the power of encouragement and perseverance is found in the account of King Asa, who led

---

69 Exodus 14:14

Judah back to the Lord after their years of idolatry. A prophet named Azariah reminded the king that the Lord was with him during this time of restoration. Azariah recalled Judah's history with the Lord and told King Asa to be strong and not to give up because his work would be rewarded. Emboldened, the king continued to reestablish Judah's relationship with God.[70]

When frustration and discouragement tempt us to lose hope, we're in danger of giving up on God's purposes. It takes the Holy Spirit to keep us from stalling, and that's especially true when we're supporting others. When someone relies on us, it's extremely clear that we're God's instrument; so it's important to depend on Him in order to stay on course. That means we must remain attentive to His voice and careful not to run ahead in our zeal to be a hero. It's foolish to create our own strategy and rush into action without first communicating with God. When we consult the One Who knows all, sees all, and has good plans, we gain wisdom. Through prayer, study, and godly counsel, we can discern and then follow the Lord's direction. His ways are successful, and we can trust Him to guide us. Then we can be like the rooftop friend and carry others along with us.

The author of the book of Hebrews also encourages us to persevere. In the first few verses of chapter twelve, we are told to step back and see our circumstances from a wider angle. Like a runner in a race, we can throw off any sin that slows us down and instead, keep pushing forward with determination. When we keep our eyes on Christ, we remember how He endured the cross and was victorious over death—for us! Through Him, we will not lose heart or become weary. The writer described our life in Christ as we persist through temptations and hardship. When we follow and focus on Jesus, He'll help us keep moving toward His goals. This definitely applies to our time on the sidelines. As we understand that there is significant purpose in every season of life, we recognize the need to keep going, never giving up on what God has called us to do.

---

70   2 Chronicles 15

The rooftop friend was willing to serve someone else. He and the other three companions were committed to doing anything so that their paralyzed friend could see Jesus. The readiness to help a friend, even in dire circumstances, is another way for us to be like Christ when we're in supportive roles. The writer of Proverbs points out important truths, saying, "One who has unreliable friends soon comes to ruin, but there is a friend who sticks closer than a brother,"[71] as well as, "A friend loves at all times, and a brother is born for a time of adversity."[72] Reliability, closeness, consistency, and aid during hardship are all gifts we have to share with the people in our lives. When we model our friendship after Christ, we find an extreme love that is selfless, faithful, and truly compassionate.

In his letter to the Romans, Paul expressed his hope to visit the Christians there so that they might "be mutually encouraged by each other's faith."[73] Later, he explained how love is expressed in action and advised readers to be devoted to one another and honor others above themselves. "Be joyful in hope, patient in affliction, faithful in prayer. Share with the Lord's people who are in need. Practice hospitality. Bless those who persecute you; bless and do not curse. Rejoice with those who rejoice; mourn with those who mourn."[74] Paul, like Jesus, instructed us to live lovingly and bear each other's burdens. Though the rooftop friends brought the paralyzed man to Jesus long before Paul wrote these words, they most certainly showed love the way he described. The paralyzed man experienced the benefits of his friends' efforts; his helpers had nothing to gain.

In Luke 6:32, Jesus asked His disciples, "If you love those who love you, what credit is that to you?" He continued to teach them to love their enemies by doing good deeds and giving without expecting anything in return. This is how we treat our opponents, family, friends, and neighbors. True love is

---

71   Proverbs 18:24
72   Proverbs 17:17
73   Romans 1:12
74   Romans 12:12-15

not transactional but an unconditional offering. We remember Jesus' example of choosing a modest seat at a banquet; and when He continued the dinner parable, He demonstrated selfless giving. He said that when we serve a meal, we shouldn't invite those who can repay our hospitality. Rather, invite those in need who can't welcome us in return. Jesus said that this will lead to blessing.

Perhaps the rooftop friends worried about the paralyzed man. They might have been concerned about his basic needs or his future. Though it seems that they would go to great lengths to help him, they were limited by their own resources and abilities. They could not make their friend walk, but they knew that Jesus could. We, too, can trust Jesus with our loved ones. While we often think about God's care in personal terms, we also find great comfort knowing that God nurtures, provides for, and protects our neighbors. When someone is in need, we can be like the rooftop friends and bring them to Jesus. This can be through prayer, encouragement, or tangible help as the hands and feet of Christ. This might look different for each person, as we're on many diverse walks of life. Sharing the goodness of God with those around us does not require us to save them. That's not our job but God's. The rooftop friends didn't heal the paralyzed man; Jesus did. Similarly, we care from the sidelines by loving like Christ, then stepping back to allow God to do His amazing work.

Matthew's version of the rooftop story tells us that when Jesus saw the faith of all five men, He said to the disabled friend, "Take heart, son; your sins are forgiven."[75] The belief of the abled men was as much part of the experience as the faith of their paralyzed friend. If someone is in trouble or sick, we should pray. "And the prayer offered in faith will make the sick person well; the Lord will raise them up. If they have sinned, they will be forgiven. Therefore confess your sins to each other and pray for each other so that you may be healed. The prayer of a righteous person is powerful and effective."[76] Healing happens in many different ways, and sometimes, God's

---

75   Matthew 9:2
76   James 5:15-16

timing leaves us with questions and doubt. Holding tight to His Word as we wait can be arduous. That makes interceding for another person an incredible sidelines gift. We might feel helpless as we watch a loved one suffer, but we're not powerless. We are strengthened by the Omnipotent One. Our steady faith can provide comfort to someone who is grasping to hold onto their own hope. God hears our prayers on behalf of others, and our faith matters.

We can aspire to be like the rooftop friend as we support our family, friends, and community. His example of perseverance and reliance on God to overcome barriers shows us how to endure challenges as we help others. The successful strategy to deliver the paralyzed friend to Jesus inspires confidence that God will handle anything obstructing our path. We won't give up but, instead, will seek God's wisdom in all of our plans. And as always, we will love as Christ loves us, striving for the good of others, despite having nothing to gain ourselves. To serve from the sidelines is a great privilege because it's there that we get to be a part of God's kingdom work. And perhaps from this vantage point, we might even see a miracle.

CHAPTER 12
Temple Merchant

Based on Matthew 21:1-17, Mark 11:15-18, and Luke 19:45-46

This is shaping up to be the busiest Passover yet, the merchant mused as he tended to yet another traveler who needed sacrificial doves. He was barely able to hear the birds' soft coos above the noise of the temple market. A cacophony of voices composed a chaotic symphony of happy greetings: sale negotiations, laughter, and parents scolding straying children before they got lost in the bustling crowd. Animals joined the chorus, unaware that they would soon be an offering. Meanwhile, the clink of coins as they were exchanged for temple currency provided a rhythm that brought everything together. It was music to the merchant's ears.

He scanned the crowd, looking for potential customers. The big spenders who could afford larger animals didn't interest him. Instead, he served those with humble budgets. Poor families chose the doves, and the merchant often agreed to deals that allowed them to purchase the sacrifice in addition to their required temple tax. After all, wasn't it better to have a small sale than no profit at all? He knew that some of the vendors and money changers were less kind, aiming to benefit as much as possible from festival observances. Others, like him, were happy to provide a service to worshippers and make just enough to pay his own taxes while supporting his family.

The arrangement worked well. Many of the Jewish people traveled great distances to celebrate Passover in Jerusalem. It wasn't practical to bring sacrificial animals along on the journey, so they needed to buy them in the city. Of course, they also brought their local currency to exchange for the shekels accepted here at the temple. Therefore, money changers joined the merchants, providing convenience to the visitors. The dove-seller could always count on abundant sales during the holy days, and he was glad to see returning customers each year. It was slightly amazing that they could find him in the middle of the tightly packed courtyard; but the buzz of the market felt alive, and the merchant was glad to be part of it.

He noticed a few people pointing across the crowd and whispering to one another. He followed their gaze and caught a glimpse of a small group of men. Though they might have seemed ordinary at first glance, the merchant recognized them—specifically the one in the middle—because he saw them yesterday during an unusual commotion. Jerusalem was always crowded at this time, which meant plenty of activity. But the day before, shouts rang out over the usual chatter when the merchant had walked toward the city gates.

"'Hosanna to the Son of David!'

'Blessed is He who comes in the name of the Lord!'

'Hosanna in the highest!'"[77]

The merchant had then turned around to see a small but noisy group assembling. Some brought freshly cut branches from nearby trees and others hurried to remove their coats, flinging them to the ground! The merchant was baffled at the sight of a man riding a donkey, whose muddy hooves stepped all over the clothing and branches. People were treating this man like a king but without the expensive honor of royalty.

As the merchant arrived at Jerusalem slightly ahead of the celebration, he wondered if they could be mocking the man. Others around him asked, "Who is this?" and tried to guess if he was someone important. Voices from

---

77   Matthew 21:9

the shouting crowd loudly answered them: "This is the prophet who came from Nazareth! You haven't heard of Jesus?"

At the mention of that name, the merchant had recalled accounts of healings and teachings he heard over the past year or so. This was the first time he had seen for himself the man that people said was the Son of God. Of course, Jesus would also honor the Passover in Jerusalem. The merchant shrugged and continued on his way. *You never know who you might see in the city this time of year.*

Now, Jesus was here in the temple market with His friends. It was too noisy for Him to teach, though the merchant had heard He had done so here before. Plenty of people in the crowd needed to be healed; but with everyone packed shoulder to shoulder, it would be difficult to make room for a miracle. Besides, it appeared that Jesus was displeased, though He was too far away for the merchant to clearly see His face.

In an instant, it became obvious that Jesus was more than unhappy. He was livid! The merchant's heart lurched as a wave of fear washed over him. Jesus pushed His way through the crowd, making deliberate strides toward the dove-selling booth. The money changer beside him looked over at the merchant, unsure of what was happening or what he should do. Before either of them could say anything, Jesus turned and approached the money changer's booth. Enraged, He abruptly overturned the entire table! Coins scattered with a clamor as they hit the ground, and the money changer scrambled to get out of the way. A few people tried to grab the loose money but were startled when Jesus loudly declared, "It is written . . . 'My house will be called a house of prayer,' but you are making it 'a den of robbers.'"[78]

Before the merchant understood what was happening, Jesus was right in front of him. The anger on his face was frightening, causing the merchant to jump behind his neighbor's upside-down table. He narrowly avoided being hit by his own bench as Jesus shoved it aside.

---

78 Matthew 21:13

Could this really be the Prophet people were happy to see? This is the healing Teacher?

The merchant's questions were pushed aside as he watched people frantically rushing away from the outburst. Nearby money changers clutched their coins and swarmed to the nearest exit. Those who sold animals secured them as quickly as possible and followed behind, slowed by the mass of fleeing people in their path. Jesus moved away from them, turning more tables while the merchant gathered his doves with shaking hands. He and the money changer hurried out of the temple market.

Well, thought the terrified merchant, *this is certainly the wildest Passover yet.*

●●●●●●●●●●●●●●●●●●●●●●●●●●●●●●●

We don't receive a path to follow or an example to imitate from the temple merchant. Instead, we are given an opportunity to ask questions about our own course. The merchant was in the wrong place at the wrong time doing the wrong thing. Yet he found himself face to face with Jesus, something that many people wanted, though this particular situation was one that they'd rather avoid. His encounter with Christ was strikingly different from the gentle healings and wise teachings we typically prefer to hear. But the Lord's anger is holy, giving us a deeper glimpse into His character. Additionally, we're given more insight into His purposes when we're on the sidelines.

To begin, we need to be familiar with the context of the story. The incident took place in the temple, specifically the courtyard where the Gentiles were permitted to worship. To accommodate the large number of people in Jerusalem for holy days, merchants and money changers offered the market as a convenient place to obtain sacrificial animals as well as the currency accepted by the temple. However, instead of being helpful, this was especially harmful. An examination of this text helps us understand why.

Many scholars have studied this passage and attempted to explain what inspired Jesus' rage. One thought is that the vendors were cheating the people, much like the tax collectors were known to do. Making a profit from worship is definitely displeasing to the Lord. However, some researchers point out that there's a lack of evidence to confirm that cheating or greed was actually happening. Another possible offense was exploitation of the poor. The focus on the dove-sellers, the option for those who couldn't afford to sacrifice a larger animal, suggests that this was what angered Jesus. But if we look at the account of clearing the market in John's Gospel, we find that it describes Jesus driving out all of the animals, including the more expensive offerings. John's description includes different details and a different timeline, so it's unclear whether he wrote about the same event or a separate incident.

An alternate idea is that the problem was disruption of the Gentiles' worship. Noise and market activity would have certainly made it difficult to focus, listen, and pray. When we consider the words that Jesus shouted, it seems that the transgression was likely location. However, it affected so much more than the Gentiles' space. Buying and selling in the temple was a symptom of greater issues.

The first part of Jesus' exclamation came from Isaiah 56:6-7. That prophecy said:

> And foreigners who bind themselves to the LORD to minister to him, to love the name of the LORD, and to be his servants, all who keep the Sabbath without desecrating it and who hold fast to my covenant—these I will bring to my holy mountain and give them joy in my house of prayer. Their burnt offerings and sacrifices will be accepted on my altar; for my house will be called a house of prayer for all nations.

This reminded the people of the temple's purpose.

Then, Jesus referenced Jeremiah 7:9-11: "Will you steal and murder, commit adultery and perjury, burn incense to Baal and follow other gods you have not known, and then come and stand before me in this house, which bears my Name, and say, 'We are safe'—safe to do all these detestable things? Has this house, which bears my Name, become a den of robbers to you? But I have been watching! declares the LORD." The people of Jeremiah's era and those who lived in Jesus' time had something in common, an issue that we might find familiar now. They disregarded the Lord in everyday life, then came to worship at the temple. Like a hiding place for thieves, they considered this a "safe" place and believed that sacrifices would cancel out their sins, allowing them to resume their habits upon returning home.

We should keep this context in mind as we look through the eyes of the temple merchant. When we place ourselves in his position, our first instinct might be to protest. After all, we would never want to make Jesus angry! And yet, even though we know the rules and do our best to follow them, we recognize that we also disobey God at times. Often it happens bit by bit, as one small choice leads to many more in the wrong direction. It's possible that some of our questions about this story will go unanswered. We don't know how the merchant responded to the incident or what he did after. We wonder what he thought about Jesus after hearing reports and imagine that perhaps he had witnessed the Lord's arrival to Jerusalem with the Passover crowd. Was the merchant changed after experiencing Jesus' outburst, or did he go back to business as usual?

These questions lead us to more personal matters. Will we recognize when God points out our own sinfulness? Will we be obedient to change or cling to stubborn defiance? When we lose our way, will we be receptive to God's correction as He points us to His purposes? Or will we ignore each opportunity to accept His forgiveness and adjust our course? The longer we resist Him, the more we delay understanding and living out His design for us. It's not easy to admit wrong, and looking at the motivation behind our sin can be painful.

Let's walk with the merchant to the best of our ability. He inspires us to ask questions that are worth pondering. How did he find himself in the middle of an angry conflict? It's likely that he arrived through a series of smaller circumstances and decisions. First, he needed to make a living, which is not wrong. However, the chance to take his business to the temple took him to sinful territory. Besides offering a service to visitors, he had the personal benefit of a good location for ample business, making the choice quite appealing. Before he knew it, he was complicit in the collective offense of misusing a holy place.

Because we are human, we can't avoid sin. Romans 3 points out that no one is righteous and that "all have sinned and fall short of the glory of God."[79] That's why we need Jesus. Meanwhile, James describes the sin process that begins with temptation. First, each person is pulled away from following God by desires that contradict His ways. When we act on these, we begin to sin. When that sin grows, we experience the consequences.[80] It happens to all of us, every day.

But there's hope because that isn't the end of our story. Christ confronted the temple merchants, and He also addresses our sins. Thankfully, it's typically gentler than overturned tables and angry shouts. We receive conviction from the Holy Spirit, words spoken by other believers, and direct instruction from Scripture. Once we become aware of our disobedience, we have the choice to pay attention to the Lord or push that awareness aside and continue doing our own thing.

In his second letter to the Corinthian church, Paul talked about their response when God revealed their sin. He referenced his first letter, which had identified some of their wrongdoings. However, Paul said that any sorrow that the letter caused was temporary, and it convicted the people to stop sinning and obediently follow God again. He explained that godly sorrow produced earnestness and eagerness to clear themselves. They were then urgently concerned and ready to see justice done.[81] We can learn from this reaction and choose to allow conviction to move us to repentance as well.

Paul had also told them in his first letter that any temptation we face is common to all people and that God will always provide a way to resist it.[82] Running toward Him instead of away is our first act of defense against sin. That may look a little different for each of us, but it must always include ample time

---

79   Romans 3:11, 23
80   Romans 1:14-15
81   2 Corinthians 7
82   1 Corinthians 10:13

in prayer. Frequently reading God's Word, connecting with a community of other believers, and serving Him in tangible ways are all part of seeking the Lord.

The temple merchant also represents collective community sin. We remember that when Jesus accused them of making God's house of prayer into a den of robbers, He referenced Jeremiah's description of Israel's sin. They disobeyed God continually, then came to worship as if that freed them from God's consequences. This is like our tendency to live daily life on our own terms, then show up at church each week. We touch base with God and get a dose of forgiveness so that we can continue to go our own way again. This is a dangerous cycle. In addition to disrespecting the Lord, repetitive sin foolishly pushes us further away from His purposes.

To start off Romans 6, Paul asks a rhetorical question: should we continue to sin so that we get more grace? He explains that of course, we shouldn't because we died to our sin when Jesus provided salvation through His death and resurrection. Instead, we live a new life in Him. We must not offer any part of ourselves to sin but rather offer ourselves to God as an instrument of righteousness because we have been brought from death to life.[83] When we love God, we follow His commands. Living as we want, checking in with God to clear our record, then resuming our sin simply does not work. We will always eventually come face-to-face with complicated consequences.

The merchant forgot the sanctity of the temple because he was distracted by day-to-day living. So often, our own sin begins with well-intentioned distractions. We remember when sisters Mary and Martha welcomed Jesus, their dear Friend, into their home. While Mary sat and listened to Him, Martha's priority was caring for Jesus through hospitality. After preparing the house and meal by herself, Martha became exasperated with her sister and appealed to Jesus, asking Him to tell Mary to help. Jesus surprised Martha by replying that Mary had chosen the better thing.[84] He showed Martha how

---

83   Romans 6:1-4
84   Luke 10:38-42

to realign her priorities, and that's where the story ends. We can only wonder about her response. Did she put aside meal prep and join her sister? If instead she continued to be more concerned with hospitality than with their guest, she could have easily allowed earthly things to come between her and Christ.

Earlier, Jesus told a parable about seeds growing in different soils; and it included the dangers of distraction. The seeds represent the Word of God, while the soil is a symbol for our hearts. One of the seeds, planted among thorns, begins to grow; but the weeds soon choke it out. Jesus said that this illustrates how worries and other interferences can choke out things of God from our hearts.[85] Similarly, the temple market began as a convenient way to serve worshippers and benefit the merchants, money changers, and those serving in the temple. They thought these were beneficial, but their choice led them away from the true purpose of God's house of prayer. When we look at ourselves, can we see if we began to stray? It's often subtle and grows slowly. Can we be brave enough to honestly identify the start of our waywardness?

Sin builds a barrier that obstructs a healthy and whole relationship with God. Just as Christ reacted passionately to the temple market, He is passionate about destroying obstacles that our sin places in our relationship with Him. We know that He'll go to extremes to destroy it, for that's exactly what He did by providing salvation through the cross. He also wants to tear down the hurdles we've constructed today. Often, this work happens on the sidelines.

These sidelines seasons are often interludes of heart repair. Though we might feel that our days are dull compared to the busy lives of people around us, we're safely in a quiet place that allows us to have one-on-one time with the Lord. Like a refining fire or the pruning of vines, it's not comfortable when God addresses our sin. The temple merchant had an intense encounter with Jesus, Who revealed the offenses of the marketplace. While we don't know how the merchant responded, we do know our own hearts. When we're brave enough to acknowledge the truth and embrace it to deal with our sin,

---

85 Mark 4:1-20

we experience God's transformation in us. Our lives are changed, and we emerge in a closer relationship with Him.

As the Lord restores us, we can once again take part in His good plans. From our previous stories, we've learned that God's direction points us to blessing. We remember our purpose when we remember Christ. Therefore, when we're firmly rooted in Him, we are right where we need to be.

The first psalm illustrates this with the image of a tree planted by water, similar to the imagery from Jeremiah that we pondered in a previous chapter. It's nourished and full of life, and so are those who delight in and meditate on God's law. However, those who turn their back on God's instruction are chaff, or husks and seeds, which blow away in the wind.[86] Jesus offered another example and said that He is the Vine, while we are the branches.[87] If branches aren't connected to vines, they don't produce fruit. We can't fulfill our purpose apart from the Lord.

It takes intentional discipline to walk with the Lord. "Let your eyes look straight ahead; fix your gaze directly before you. Give careful thought to the paths for your feet and be steadfast in all your ways. Do not turn to the right or the left; keep your foot from evil."[88] Avoiding sin is not a passive habit; it's an active pursuit of Christ. No matter what stage of life we happen to be in, being securely grounded in Him is vital.

Hopefully, the temple merchant was changed that day. As we look at our reaction when God shows us our disobedience, we realize that it's a kindness when the Lord places us in a season of repentance and we experience His forgiveness. He overturns the tables of sin we put in our lives so that we can abandon our defiance and return to His goodness.

---

86 Psalm 1:1-3
87 John 15
88 Proverbs 4:25-27

CHAPTER 13
Matthias

Based on Acts 1-2

They were still getting used to the idea that Jesus was alive. He had proven many times that it was true, as He had frequently appeared during the month since His crucifixion and resurrection. Earlier, He had encouraged His disciples and followers while they shared a meal, telling them more about the kingdom of God. It was good to sit with their Friend and Teacher, something previously quite normal that had become a wonder after His return to life. One follower, Matthias, listened intently as Jesus spoke to them.

"Stay in Jerusalem," He instructed, "and be patient for the promised gift from my Father Remember that John baptized with water; but soon, the Holy Spirit will baptize you.

Maybe this would be when the Lord restored the kingdom to Israel! Before they became overly excited, Jesus reminded them that it wasn't for them to know when that would happen. There were important things for them to do first.

Jesus gently told them, "The Holy Spirit will come upon you, and then you'll testify about Me here and throughout the world."

Matthias wondered what that would be like. Could it be similar to the ability God had once given them to make sick people well?

Jesus sent them ahead of Him in pairs to various towns without even a bag or sandals. They stayed in friendly homes, told communities about the Kingdom of God, and healed those who were ill. It astounded Matthias to be filled with God's power! When they returned, he enthusiastically told Jesus about his experience, marveling that even demons submitted to the name of the Lord.

But at this moment, something was changing. They had gathered outside, continuing their conversation while enjoying fresh air. Matthias suddenly realized that Jesus was rising off the ground! He had seen many miracles as a follower for the past three years, but this was new. What was happening?

Matthias kept his eyes on Jesus, straining his neck and shading his eyes from the light as their Teacher continued to move toward the heavens. He didn't want to blink and lose sight of Jesus in the glaring sun. It wasn't until a cloud obstructed their view of Him that Matthias realized that two men dressed in white were standing among the disciples and followers.

One of the strangers spoke. "Why are you still looking at the clouds? Jesus has now gone from you and into Heaven. He will one day return in the same way." The disciples and followers remembered all that they had seen and the many things that Jesus told them. They knew the stranger was right. It was time to return to Jerusalem.

The followers met together frequently to pray, worship, and discuss how they would fulfill the Lord's instructions. There were about 120 of them gathered one day when Peter stood up and spoke.

"Brothers and sisters, it's time for Scripture to be fulfilled after Judas, who was one of our own, betrayed Jesus. Now we must fill his place among those chosen to be the Lord's apostles. It must be one of the men who've been present the whole time Jesus was here, from His baptism to the time when He ascended. This man must have witnessed the resurrection with us."

After thoughtful discussion, the believers decided that there were two men who could serve well. They first called Justus to stand, and then they said the name "Matthias." Matthias could feel his heart beating fiercely in his chest as Peter explained what would happen next: they would seek God's will for this critical decision.

The believers joined Peter as he led them in prayer. "Lord, you are familiar with every heart in this room. Please show us whom You choose to be part of Your ministry as an apostle."

Another apostle stepped forward holding a small jar that rattled with two stones inside. Matthias knew that one represented him and the other Justus, and whichever they poured out first would receive the honor of becoming an ambassador of the Lord. The room was silent as the apostle shook the jar. Slowly and deliberately, he tipped the opening toward the table. Matthias was simultaneously dumbfounded and exhilarated to see his stone emerge first. He barely registered the encouragement of the other believers as he took in what this meant. After years of wondering what it would be like to be in Jesus' inner circle, he would now join the eleven apostles to take the message of Christ to Jerusalem, Judea, Samaria, and even the ends of the earth.

From that moment and until Pentecost, Matthias spent a great deal of time with the other apostles. When he was alone, he alternated between fervent prayer and recalling each moment he'd had with Jesus. He would never forget hearing the voice of God declaring that Jesus was His beloved Son as John the Baptist brought Jesus up from the water of the Jordan River.

The next three years were a blur, full of crowds seeking healing and treasured moments between the Teacher and followers who stayed beside Him when the masses returned home. Matthias witnessed sight restored, disabilities transformed, and demons cast out. He knew about a calmed storm, a walk on the sea, and even the dead being raised. Through discussions filled with parables, Matthias better understood God's compassion, law, and kingdom. He grew to love Jesus dearly, which made His devastatingly cruel death on the cross nearly impossible for Matthias to bear. Yet only days later, he was overwhelmed with exceeding joy as he attempted to comprehend Jesus' resurrection. Yes, the Lord had told them that this would happen, but Matthias was not truly prepared. He couldn't fathom how anyone would doubt that Jesus was God's Son after all that had occurred. The evidence was clear, and Matthias would remain a dedicated follower until his final breath. He would step into his new role as the twelfth apostle so that all could know about his dear Teacher and Friend.

As the day of Pentecost arrived, the believers gathered once again to pray and worship. It seemed to be like most meetings, until a sudden sound, almost like a windstorm, filled the entire place! Matthias looked over at Peter and saw something like a tongue of fire settling on him. Then he noticed that flames were upon the other apostles! Looking around the room, Matthias saw that each believer also had the tongue of fire above them, and he knew that he did as well. A feeling beyond description overcame him. Somehow, the believers knew that this was the Holy Spirit that Jesus told them would come. As they opened their mouths to praise God, they began to exclaim in many other languages! Wide-eyed at this phenomenon, the believers were emboldened by the Spirit and confidently proclaimed their praise to God with words they had never known before.

Voices from outside the house joined the shouts. A crowd of Jews from various nations congregated around the house, all amazed at what they were hearing. They couldn't imagine how a group of people from Galilee could be speaking to them in their native languages, telling them about the kingdom of God! Some were perplexed and suggested that perhaps the believers were merely drunk. Peter immediately stood with the other apostles and addressed the crowd so that they could understand what was happening.

Matthias knew that Peter's words were of the Spirit as he explained that, of course, the believers had not been drinking. It was still morning! He reminded them all that Joel's prophecy said that God's Spirit would be poured out and told the signs that were to come. Then Peter spoke about

Jesus, demonstrating how He fulfilled the Scriptures, was resurrected, and was the Messiah. His speech moved the hearts of the people, and they eagerly followed Peter's instructions to repent of their sins and be baptized in the name of Jesus. They were promised that they, too, would receive the incredible gift of the Holy Spirit. Approximately three thousand people were inspired to join the believers of Christ.

A new era had arrived. Matthias and the apostles missed the days they walked with Jesus, but they treasured the presence of the Holy Spirit, their Helper and Advocate. They were ready to take the Good News of the Lord to all, making disciples and baptizing them in the name of the Father, the Son, and the Holy Spirit. They would teach them to obey everything that Jesus had commanded, trusting that He was with them always, to the very end of time.

● ●

For three years, Matthias faithfully followed Christ without knowing that he would be appointed as an apostle—a messenger or ambassador for Jesus. He witnessed many incredible things, while hearing about others from Peter, James, and John. Since Matthias is never mentioned in Scripture outside of a few verses in Acts 1, we know almost nothing about him. Scholars speculate that he was likely one of the seventy-two followers Jesus sent out in Luke 10, but there are no verified lists to confirm this. However, based on Peter's qualifications for Judas' replacement, we do know that Matthias was present throughout Jesus' ministry and witnessed His resurrection.

Though the first two chapters of Acts are frequently read and often taught in Bible studies, most of us miss or forget Justus and Matthias. Yet they were respected and trusted by the eleven apostles and the other followers of Christ. Specially chosen, Matthias was given the responsibility and privilege of serving the Lord in an important position. This was an extremely big deal that is often neglected by modern attention. But when we consider Matthias, we're reminded that there's often more to most stories than what we initially see. Our observations aren't always complete, and we discover additional details with a second look. It also inspires us to pursue deeper Bible study than what we might take in during a sermon or podcast. This provides an opportunity to learn more than what we might hear in the time constraints of any single teaching. The potential for deeper understanding should motivate us to seek a complete story in the context of Scripture.

Matthias also helps us remember that the perceptions of a crowd don't accurately measure our significance. We may perceive that celebrities or public figures are special because they have greater prominence than the average citizen. We can be fooled by the illusion of photos and news releases, forgetting that even the most well-known person is ordinary under all the fuss. As we've been reminded in previous sidelines stories, we often mistakenly use popularity as a metric for success. It becomes an incorrect indication of value, a false measurement of worth. Yet despite only a small mention in the text, Matthias was an integral part of spreading the gospel and growing the church. To the average reader, he seems to be a minor character; but to everyone he encountered and encouraged, he was the hands and feet of Christ. God can also do the same through us when eagerly seek to serve! This radically changes how we approach ourselves and others.

The example Matthias sets is one of faithful service for the sake of loving the Lord. Despite not being chosen as one of the twelve disciples at the beginning of Jesus' ministry, Matthias remained devoted. This long-term dedication, combined with God's favor in selecting him for apostleship, demonstrates that his heart was primarily motivated by love for Christ. His interest in Jesus' teachings persisted even after the short attention span of most of the crowds. Additionally, his years following Jesus prepared him for his specific role as the twelfth apostle. God's timing is perfect, and our sidelines seasons are frequently intended to be preparation for future situations and callings. Our purpose is often to meet a specific need, just like Matthias; and the Lord leads us through necessary experiences to equip us for His service. When Matthias wasn't enjoying the privileges of the closer twelve disciples, was Jesus teaching him humility? Perhaps when he and the other seventy-one followers went out ahead of Jesus, he met specific people who would be key in his future ministry. Maybe he saw things differently than the twelve who spent more time with Jesus, and he viewed miracles and teachings from another angle.

God utilizes every part of our journey, and His timing is intentional. Peter explained this in his second letter, addressing the Lord's return. He wrote, "The Lord is not slow in keeping his promise, as some understand slowness. Instead he is patient with you, not wanting anyone to perish, but everyone to come to repentance."[89] Though we eagerly anticipate when Jesus comes again, it's God's great love that establishes His schedule. We can't always see this with our limited view, but we can trust that His reasons are good. This aspect of His timing isn't only for the Second Coming. We read in the third chapter of Ecclesiastes that God appoints a time for everything and then He makes it all beautiful.

If every season has a specific purpose and God transforms everything into beauty, we can be encouraged that the occasions we feel are less significant are, in fact, essential to His plan. We might think we're waiting in the wings; but God is developing our gifts, skills, and understanding. He is getting us ready for the next act. We can see this process in other biblical accounts before we read about Matthias. Moses spent years as a shepherd before he was ready to lead the Israelites. Esther had over a year of preparation before she became a queen and found herself in a position to save God's people. Likewise, the disciples had to grow from fishermen or tax collectors into apostles, despite a lack of formal training in speaking or writing. Their time with Jesus equipped them perfectly.

It's easy to think that the twelve disciples were extra special because they get a great deal of attention in the Gospels. But we can also assume that Jesus knew Matthias well. After all, if Matthias was around so often, Jesus would have become his Friend, too. He valued Matthias; and as the Son

---

89 2 Peter 3:9

of God, He would have known that Matthias would eventually become an apostle after His ascension. However, Jesus didn't love Matthias because he was extraordinary. Matthias was a regular guy who loved the Lord. Christ treasures us each individually and pays attention to us even when it seems that no one else sees us. It doesn't matter who else remembers Matthias because His beloved Teacher loved him dearly. We can have confidence in that by examining the way God cares for each of us.

David wrote a beautiful song that we now call Psalm 139. He sang about how intricately God knows us, contemplating that the Lord searches us and is familiar with each of our actions, even simple things like getting up or sitting down. God knows what we are going to say before we say it; and He is always with us, no matter how far we think we might venture away from Him. He created every intricate part of us and knew us even before our mothers felt our first kicks.

His love is not limited, nor does it have an expiration date. In God's Word, through Jeremiah's prophecy, He told the people of Israel just how long He would care for them. "The Lord appeared to us in the past, saying: 'I have loved you with an everlasting love; I have drawn you with unfailing kindness.'"[90] In a message through the prophet Zephaniah, God's people are encouraged with specific ways He cares for them. He said that God is "the Mighty Warrior who saves. He will take great delight in [them] . . . love [them] . . . [and] rejoice over [them] with singing."[91] We know that we can cherish these ancient words as well because God's loving character is consistent forever, and we became part of His family through Jesus. Paul explained that "The Spirit you received brought about your adoption to sonship. And by him we cry, 'Abba, Father.' The Spirit himself testifies with our spirit that we are God's children."[92]

We can be confident that Jesus loved Matthias and that He similarly cares for us. Nothing can separate us from His love, which is often beyond our

---

90   Jeremiah 31:3
91   Zephaniah 3:17
92   Romans 8:15-16

comprehension. Paul's prayer for the Ephesian church is also for us today. He wrote, "I pray that you, being rooted and established in love, may have power, together with all the Lord's holy people, to grasp how wide and long and high and deep is the love of Christ, and to know this love that surpasses knowledge—that you may be filled to the measure of all the fullness of God."[93] God is not limited in His affections. When we feel forgotten by the people around us, we can be certain that He remembers us, and His compassion envelops us completely. We don't need earthly praise but instead to be secure in the Lord's gaze. He promises that His eyes will always be on us.

With increased knowledge of God's love, let's glance once more at Matthias' story. When Jesus lived on earth, the twelve disciples were closest to Him. We wonder if Matthias ever felt like an outsider around them; and we can imagine his emotions when he was welcomed into that group, chosen to be an apostle. Maybe he felt a sense of belonging, or it might have been hard to believe that he was included. We don't know exactly what Matthias was thinking, but we do know what it's like to be welcomed by Christ. Yes, Jesus welcomes us to be close to Him, too. Despite how we might perceive His relationship with the disciples, He doesn't have favorites. He wants to be near each one of us.

We get a glimpse of this truth during an incident with Jesus' biological family. He was speaking to a crowd in a house, and his mother, Mary, and his brothers waited outside to talk to Him. Someone got Jesus' attention and told Him that His family was there to see Him.

Jesus' reply likely surprised them all. "He replied to him, 'Who is my mother, and who are my brothers?' Pointing to his disciples, he said, 'Here are my mother and my brothers. For whoever does the will of my Father in heaven is my brother and sister and mother.'"[94] Jesus wasn't rejecting His family; He cared deeply for them. However, He accepts into His family all those who love Him, which includes His followers today. His great care for

93 Ephesians 3:17-19
94 Matthew 12:48-50

any one person doesn't leave less for another. The love of Christ is limitless with an overflowing abundance of compassion for each of us.

Like Matthias, we're invited to be near the Lord. At the end of the book of Revelation, we are also called to Him. After John shared the vision of Heaven from God, these words were given to all who read and heard it: "The Spirit and the bride say, 'Come!' And let the one who hears say, 'Come!' Let the one who is thirsty come; and let the one who wishes take the free gift of the water of life."[95] The invitation to be close to Christ wasn't only for people who were with Him when He was on earth. He welcomes us today and will continue to welcome us through eternity.

When it seems like we're on the outside of the crowd looking in, it can be easy to feel like we're unimportant or loved less than others. Matthias shows us that this isn't true. Our road to understanding and fulfilling God's purpose doesn't look like anyone else's, but what we all have in common is the everlasting love of Christ. There aren't really any idle moments because each minute on the sidelines prepares us for the astounding things God has waiting for us. He draws us close and stays with us in every season, making it all beautiful in His perfect time.

---

95   Revelation 22:17

CHAPTER 14
Apollos

Based on Acts 18, 1 Corinthians 1-4, 16:12, and Titus 3:13

The minute he stepped into the bustling port city of Ephesus, Apollos felt his confidence falter. This was unexpected; typically, he stood with great self-assurance in front of crowds and easily won debates. Years of training from the acclaimed speakers in the Egyptian city of Alexandria equipped Apollos with expert rhetorical skills. His studies had filled him with knowledge of nearly every topic, and he knew how to deliver his arguments with passionate conviction. Of course, Apollos valued listening as well. The opportunity to learn from experts and philosophers inspired him to stay sharp, informed, and ready for any discussion. He was well-respected in Alexandria, but it was time to embark on the next adventure. Now he walked among the crowded streets of a new city, eager to know it better but uncertain about how he would be received.

Of all the subjects he had studied, Apollos was most enthralled by reading the Scriptures of his Jewish heritage, the laws and prophecies of the God of Israel. He was intrigued by the foretelling of the coming Messiah; so when he heard about a man in Judea claiming to prepare the way of the Lord, he had to know more. Apollos learned that this man, named John, preached in the wilderness and baptized people as a sign of repentance from their sins. Word also spread about a teacher named Jesus Who performed miracles, healed people, and claimed to be the Son of God. Apollos applied everything he knew about the Scriptures and believed that this was indeed the Messiah.

Ever the diligent student, Apollos dedicated himself to the way of the Lord. The more knowledge he gained, the more eager he was to share. He left Egypt, and his travels brought him to Ephesus. As he settled in, he met other followers of God who welcomed him into their community. Before long, Apollos was invited to speak in the synagogue; and the people were captivated by his enthusiastic teaching. Any decrease in his confidence was long forgotten. Apollos knew how to speak well, and he strongly believed that what he taught was true. He wanted everyone to know the Good News of the Messiah, and he hoped it would encourage them to believe as well.

After a lengthy speech one afternoon, Apollos stepped out of the synagogue and onto the sunlit street. A man and a woman quickly approached him. The man spoke first.

"Greetings. My name is Aquila, and this is my wife, Priscilla. We heard your exceptional discourse today and wanted to meet you."

Priscilla added, "We would be honored if you would join us in our home, perhaps to continue the conversation about the Messiah."

At that moment, Apollos was unaware that his new friends had something incredible to share. Their discussion became pleasantly animated before they even reached the house. There was so much more to learn about Jesus than Apollos realized.

For hours, the three talked about the Scriptures and the things Jesus had done. Then, Priscilla asked a question that Apollos couldn't answer.

"Do you know about the arrival of the Holy Spirit?"

The couple must have seen the mix of confusion, surprise, and intrigue on Apollos' face; but he didn't allow the stunned silence to remain for long.

"What do you mean?" Apollos asked. "Did we miss something in Alexandria?"

Indeed, they had. Apollos listened intently as Aquila and Priscilla recounted Jesus' final days on earth after His resurrection. They told him what Jesus had said about a Helper and Advocate Who would come after His departure. The next part was even more amazing; the dramatic experience of Jesus' followers during Pentecost was nearly beyond Apollos' imagination. He now understood even better than before! Jesus truly was the Messiah, and the presence and power of God's Holy Spirit transformed Apollos' mind as well as his heart.

The realization that there was more to learn humbled Apollos' pride in his own teaching abilities. He had stood before crowds with such certainty, but now he realized that he had done the people a disservice by being inadequately educated. His many years in elite schools of Alexandria didn't prepare him for Priscilla and Aquila's instruction. Still, Apollos was not discouraged. This correction opened his eyes with new insight. He also wanted to experience the Holy Spirit; and then he would tell everyone he could that Jesus was indeed the Messiah, and there was more to prove it. He was truly the Son of God, deserving of all thanks and praise and worthy of their discipleship as they lived in the Spirit.

The church in Ephesus grew and was strengthened in the time that followed. Apollos became a beloved leader as he used his rhetorical skills to share the complete gospel message. The believers were heartened by this and applied what they learned to their daily lives. But his season there was coming to an end. Apollos felt that God was leading him somewhere new, across the sea to the Greek city of Corinth. Though the Ephesian church community would greatly miss him, they encouraged him to share his knowledge and talents with the people there. Together, they penned a written introduction to the Corinthian disciples and urged them to welcome their beloved teacher. After heartfelt goodbyes, Apollos traveled again.

Corinth seemed a bit like Alexandria, so Apollos felt at home rather quickly. The people here also valued philosophy, knowledge, and debate. It didn't take long for him to demonstrate his skill and intelligence, and he soon earned respect from many of the people. After his initial welcome into the Corinthian church, he proved to be an uplifting and valuable leader. When Jewish opponents wanted to disprove his faith in Jesus through reason and arguments, Apollos matched their skill. He clearly showed how the Scriptures confirmed that Jesus was the Messiah.

Talented speakers were admired for their rhetoric here. People devoted themselves to their favorite orator, becoming competitive with those who preferred different teachers. After some time, Apollos knew he must move on and share his gifts with other church communities. As he traveled, he finally met the apostle Paul, friend of Aquila and Priscilla, and they shared stories of their ministries while encouraging one another. Paul also brought news of Apollos' friends in Corinth. There had been division among the believers regarding loyalty to their teachers. Some zealously claimed to follow Apollos, while others argued that Paul was the superior leader. The dispute became a full-blown quarrel, prompting Paul to remind them that they were not to follow either human teacher but that their devotion should be directed to God alone. Paul's work in establishing the church was like planting a seed. When Apollos arrived to help them, it was similar to watering it. However, as only God can make plants grow, so only Christ was the Foundation and Center of the Church.

"They asked for you to return," Paul added. "I think it would be good if you did."

But after prayerful thought, Apollos declined. "Now is not the time, but I hope to return at a better opportunity."

So Apollos continued to travel, taking the Word of the Lord to every community he visited. No longer did nerves creep in, as they had upon his arrival in Ephesus. Nor was his confidence rooted in his well-practiced speaking techniques. He was empowered by the Holy Spirit, an instrument of God's momentous work.

●●●●●●●●●●●●●●●●●●●●●●●●●●●●●●●●

How did Apollos truly feel about his skills, or what was it like to learn from Priscilla and Aquila? Once again, we only have basic facts before the narrative moves on, leaving us to imagine how we might have reacted in his situation. The things we do know about Apollos give us substantial insight, especially about how God directs us while we guide other people. Often, we don't think of a teacher as a sideline-dweller. However, following the Christ-like model of servant leadership moves us from being the center of attention to practicing encouragement alongside others. Using Jesus' modest service as an example, we can put aside the notion that we're superior simply because we hold a leadership position. It's possible to be a guide while living beside our neighbors in equality, and doing so can make us more effective as leaders.

Apollos seemed to be a well-grounded teacher. He doesn't receive much notoriety in Scripture, but his role in the early church was significant. Without excessive pride, he was willing to continue learning. Extensive education and impressive rhetorical skills set him apart from many others; but soon, he moved from being an instructor to becoming a student. He demonstrated that teachability is crucial for our growth and beneficial to those around us. Not only is it vital for our own character development, it's also one of the responsibilities of leadership. Learning equips us to lead well. A willingness to be taught extinguishes arrogance, which can hinder our growth if allowed to burn freely like a wildfire. Meanwhile, an eagerness to learn fosters the kind of humility that's essential to following God and living in community. If we resist education because we think we've mastered everything, we will be held back from obtaining true wisdom. In fact, it makes us foolish.

We must never stop being educated. Proverbs 9:9 advises, "Instruct the wise and they will be wiser still; teach the righteous and they will add to their learning." There is always more wisdom to attain! Being teachable keeps us from becoming complacent and mistakenly believing that we've reached the height of our knowledge. This matters in a leadership position where we can easily feel as though we've advanced to a level where we exclusively dispense information and no longer need to obtain it. Leading without learning is like trying to continuously pour from a cup without refilling it. Thankfully, we're given opportunities for growth during sidelines seasons. It doesn't matter if what we learn equips us for personal experiences or if the knowledge is intended to be shared with someone else; it has the potential to increase our God-given wisdom. A teachable attitude is developed on the sidelines so that we, like Apollos, can move forward with God's purpose for our lives.

The story of Philip and the Ethiopian is another beautiful example of intelligent men who received more instruction. An important official from Ethiopia was returning from worshiping God in Jerusalem. As his chariot rolled down the road toward home, he studied Scripture—specifically Isaiah's prophecy. Meanwhile, God had directed Philip, a follower of Christ, to travel down the same road. Philip encountered the official and caught up with the moving chariot. He asked the official if he understood what he was reading, and the official replied that he needed someone to explain it.

Philip began with what was written in Isaiah and explained the Good News about Jesus, which inspired the official to be baptized. Both Philip and the Ethiopian official were familiar with the ways of the Lord, yet they both had something to learn that day. The official's studies, combined with Philip's instruction, led to increased knowledge of Christ. Philip knew the gospel; but as he followed the prompting of the Holy Spirit, he saw God transform someone outside of Israel. This likely furthered his understanding of God's plan as well.[96]

As our own wisdom develops, so does our maturity. God continuously develops our character; and maturing is necessary for our own sake, as well as for those we lead, influence, or simply encounter. Apollos demonstrated this when he recognized that the people's devotion to him was unhealthy. It might have been enticing to enjoy the popularity, but instead, he kept his eyes on ministry and followed God's direction to serve other churches. His

---

96 Acts 8:26-40

spiritual maturity kept his pride in check and redirected the Corinthians to worship God instead of a human teacher.

In his letter to the Ephesians, Paul explained that leaders of the church were given by Christ to equip people for service. They help the church body to become mature, growing in the fullness of the Lord.[97] We're not intended to remain stagnant but to spend our lifetime aiming to be more like Christ. Maturity is a perpetual ambition! Our time on the sidelines gives us an excellent opportunity to prayerfully seek and follow the Lord, then to continually increase our spiritual maturity. We can be inspired by Paul's example in Philippians 3:12-14, where he described pursuing the prize of God calling him heavenward in Christ. Despite Paul's credentials, experience, and faithfulness, he had not yet obtained that goal; but he was committed to the lifelong pursuit. Similarly, we press on toward spiritual growth with God's help. Setbacks, difficulties, and trials are all experiences that strengthen us; and we often don't realize how much we're maturing during these seasons. And even when we think that nothing is happening in our lives, the Lord is doing exceedingly much within us.

Sometimes, recognizing how far we still need to grow can be discouraging. We see our flaws and mistakes, and we might become convinced that these must be repaired before we can be part of God's plan. The longer we stare at these faults, the more we might wonder if there's any hope for us at all. However, imperfections aren't deal-breakers; we're merely in the process of God's refinement. Apollos was highly educated, but he still needed improvement because he lacked knowledge of the subject he passionately taught. No amount of his own effort could prepare him to serve well; but the Lord guided his steps, equipped him with talent, developed his skills, and then provided opportunities to increase wisdom and understanding. During this process, God had purpose for Apollos as he taught Scripture and told people about Jesus. Apollos' imperfections might even have helped some receive his message.

---

97 Ephesians 4:11-13

Feeling vulnerable about our imperfections is uncomfortable, but our transparency invites others to step out of their own insecurity. They can be inspired by our example to learn something new, too. If someone as educated as Apollos still had much to learn, then it was also acceptable for anyone to have questions and seek more knowledge. We don't have to be ashamed of our flaws. This is because we are works-in-progress, walking with God and encouraging others along the way.

We also don't need to wait until God perfects us before we understand our purpose. Often, our struggles are part of what He has in mind. When we feel helpless, God's help does what we can't. When He meets our needs, it becomes a part of our lived experience that's visible to others. Our human limitations contrast with God's infinite love, clearly displaying His work that accomplishes more than our own efforts. This is explored in 2 Corinthians 12:9 when Paul shared his experience. He said that God's grace was enough because His power is evident in our weaknesses. Therefore, we can boast about our hardships because Christ's power is in us, making us strong in our weakness.

With this perspective, we can view our imperfections as building blocks instead of obstacles. We aren't stuck, even when it feels as though we are. When we consider past and present spiritual heroes, we often have the impression that only special people are useful to the Lord or that being equipped for a purpose means that we must be flawless. This is far from the truth! Every person that we see in the spotlight is just as ordinary as those who feel like they're sidekicks or spectators. We're all human beings with limited abilities. Like the Corinthians who followed Apollos, when we put anyone on a pedestal, we're admiring the wrong hero. God is the One Who is extraordinary, and we are all participants in His incredible work. God can do a lot with our difficulties, and our faults can be transformed into assets in His big-picture plan.

Apollos also demonstrated the importance of utilizing our skills for the Lord's purposes. His high-class education in Alexandria placed him in the mainstream arena of philosophy and debate. Yet he also loved the Lord, and his passion for studying led him to a dedicated examination of Scripture. His gift of rhetoric equipped him to teach effectively and reach an audience who might have ignored untrained speakers. Apollos was able to successfully debate opponents who wanted to disprove the Christian faith, something that required belief and knowledge as well as mastery of public speaking techniques.

Our skills that are valuable in mainstream life also give God glory as part of His kingdom work. We don't need to compartmentalize our activities into categories of "sacred" and "secular," keeping our beliefs separate from our public lives. Though we are, in many ways, different from others because we follow Christ, we're still part of the world around us. Existing as if we're in a bubble limits our ability to love those who differ from us. When we attempt to live as God instructs, we might unintentionally find ourselves in spaces that separate us from many of our neighbors. However, we always have the opportunity to bring the love of Christ to our surrounding community. Anyone, anywhere, can be blessed when we share our God-given gifts.

The Lord's purpose is not exclusive to church activities, and our mainstream happenings aren't exempt from His plans. His design is intertwined in every aspect of our diverse lives. This is true even when we're unaware or don't understand what God has in mind. Therefore, doing all things in Christ's love will always be a good decision, as the possibilities to see and share His goodness are limitless. Integrating mainstream skills with our faith opens doors. The people of Corinth valued rhetoric, and Apollos' background allowed him to communicate the gospel in a manner that they easily understood.

In our varied and colorful world, we can connect with others who share our distinct talents and interests. God has a purpose for our jobs, schools, the skills passed down from our families, and even what we learn from books or video tutorials. Relating to people through common ground is meaningful and real, providing opportunities that we would otherwise miss.

Our differences have value, too. We each understand concepts in various ways, so it takes assorted communication methods to share the goodness of God. Part of our purpose includes applying our individuality to bless anyone who might need to hear the message exactly the way we say it. Jesus called us the "'light of the world,'" just like a city 'on a hill cannot be hidden.'"[98] Lights aren't made to be covered but instead to be placed where everyone can see. God's love is meant to be expressed lavishly in every part of our lives.

God took Apollos out of Alexandria and into many communities for a reason. It wasn't because Apollos' rhetorical technique made him special, though it was a tool that helped him share the gospel. God didn't choose him to be a leader because he had achieved perfection. Instead, a teachable spirit allowed Apollos to connect with new friends and opened the door for much more than he expected. His obedience touched countless lives, both directly and through the ripple effect of people sharing what they learned from him. Thousands of years after his death, we still learn from Apollos. His example inspires us to trust that God has equipped us to extend His love to the people He places in our paths.

---

98 Matthew 5:14

CHAPTER 15
The Women of the Early Church

Based on Acts 16:11-15 & 40, Acts 18, Romans 16, 1 Corinthians
1:11, 1 Corinthians 16:19, Colossians 4:15, and 1 Timothy 4:19

LYDIA

Water rolled gently over smooth rocks, peacefully singing its own song as
the women worshiped. Lydia felt her shoulders release tension as she focused
on prayer. She was glad to put aside never-ending business matters that
required her constant attention and instead center her thoughts on sacred
practices. This was the Sabbath, the day of rest dedicated to God. The textile
trade could wait until she resumed work tomorrow. On this day, her attention
was solely devoted to the Lord.

The snap of a breaking stick was followed by the rustle of footsteps in the
weeds. The women paused their prayers as a small group of unfamiliar men
approached the riverbank. They were not often interrupted here in this quiet
spot outside of Philippi. Thankfully, the men appeared to be friendly.

"My name is Paul, a servant of Christ Jesus," the leader said. "This is Silas,
Timothy, and Luke. May we join you?"

Lydia stepped forward.

"Welcome. Yes, please sit." The women introduced themselves, welcomed
their visitors, and prepared to resume worship.

"Can you tell us more about Jesus the Messiah?" Lydia asked. Paul smiled and eagerly began to tell them about God's Son, Who healed people and taught them about His kingdom. He explained how Jesus died on a cross but returned to life again. The women were amazed, and Paul continued speaking about salvation for those who believed. Lydia was captivated. Something in her heart knew that he spoke the truth.

"I do believe!" Lydia exclaimed. "And I'd like to be baptized."

Paul agreed. Days later, Lydia brought her household to the river. As she learned more about Jesus, her enthusiasm increased. She shared the Good News with friends and family, and now she was ready to spread the Word to their community. After Paul baptized the new believers, Lydia, with hair still damp from the river, approached him with an invitation.

"As a believer in the Lord, I invite you to come and stay with me in my home." With some persuasion, Paul and his companions agreed. They were thankful for Lydia's hospitality, and their friendship began to grow. They learned that she was a successful dealer of luxurious purple cloth from across the sea in Thyatira, and she eagerly listened to tales of their travels. The once-unfamiliar men were now regularly welcomed into Lydia's house, and she delighted in being part of a growing community of Christ-followers. She opened her heart to the Lord and her home to serve His people.

PRISCILLA

It was late when the last guest left. Priscilla's body was tired, but her mind was alive from the exhilaration of the evening's discussion. She never grew weary of hosting their brothers and sisters in Christ, spending hours talking about Jesus and the ways of God. Spirituality combined with intellect; and no matter how much she studied, there was so much more she was eager to understand. Her love of learning couldn't be contained, which made Priscilla an exceptional teacher. Over the years, she instructed countless people, helping to build churches and encouraging believers to grow in their faith.

Years ago, she couldn't have imagined her life as it was now. Home had been in Rome with her husband, Aquila. They were happy there, until the emperor Claudius ordered all the Jews to leave for political reasons. What would've happened if they had stayed in Rome? They might never have traveled to Corinth, and perhaps would not have met their friend, Paul. Priscilla now knew that the Lord led them each step of the way, and that each stop on their journey was meaningful.

She and Aquila were tentmakers, something they had in common with Paul. They soon discovered further mutual interests, including a belief in Jesus. Paul told them about his encounter with Christ on his way to Damascus years before and recounted stories about his current ministry. He now lived with Priscilla and Aquila, allowing the three to work together during the day and enjoy inspiring conversations each night. The more they shared, the more Priscilla learned and the more equipped she was to teach. When it was time for Paul to travel again, the couple accompanied him, eventually arriving in Ephesus. Priscilla and Aquila established themselves in the city and immediately shared the gospel with the people there.

They remained in Ephesus even after Paul moved on and soon met a talented orator from Alexandria. His name was Apollos, and he, too, loved God with a zeal that matched Aquila and Priscilla's passionate enthusiasm. The first time the couple heard him speak, they were impressed with his intelligence and the way he clearly communicated truths about the Lord. However, something was lacking. He knew that Jesus was the Messiah, but he left out so much about His grace and salvation. It also seemed that news of the arrival of the Holy Spirit hadn't reached Apollos in his home city of Alexandria.

That was the beginning of another precious friendship. Priscilla and Aquila welcomed Apollos into their home and taught him about these crucial missing pieces. They urged Apollos to keep teaching; and together, they helped lead the church in Ephesus. Their partnership continued until God led their ministries in different directions.

Through the years, Priscilla and Aquila moved from place to place, teaching wherever they went. Each new person they met gave Priscilla a fresh opportunity to share the message of Christ. They occasionally reconnected with old friends, including Paul and others they loved dearly. Establishing churches and openly talking about Jesus could be dangerous. The couple remembered Paul's harrowing stories about the difficulties of serving God and soon found themselves in similar trouble. With persistence, they survived, knowing that God was with them during peril and had helped them to safety.

Priscilla's thoughts returned to the present, and she smiled as she reflected on all that she and Aquila had experienced. Whether welcoming neighbors into their home for worship or venturing into a new city to talk about Jesus, they were the Lord's dedicated servants. As she blew out her lamp, Priscilla knew she would never grow weary of sharing God's great love and the gifts He had given her.

NYMPHA

At a house in Laodicea, brothers and sisters gathered in the name of the Lord. The glow of lamplight and the aroma of a delicious meal surrounded them while they prayed, sang, and worshiped together. Nympha was honored that they chose her home for their regular meetings, and she wanted to provide more than a place to congregate. With care, she encouraged the believers in their pursuit of Christ. Nympha's faithfulness was a gift to their community and an important part of the Laodicean church.

PHOEBE

Despite the great number of people huddled together, the room was incredibly quiet. No one wanted to miss a word of Paul's letter that was filled with wise instruction. Phoebe stood near the door, watching the Roman Christ-followers as they listened to the reading. She had brought the letter to their church, and she hoped to help them while she was there. Her experience might be useful, as she was a deacon of the church in Cenchreae. Perhaps her long journey would benefit their community, and God would make her a blessing to them.

As a deacon, Phoebe ministered to the people, working to help them maintain their unity and to develop spiritual maturity. This position required a person to be honest and worthy of respect. A deacon must know and hold tight to the truths of their faith while having a clear conscience. Phoebe had started with basic responsibilities and grew into this demanding and honorable role. But she knew that no person could do this work alone. She was thankful for their community in Cenchreae, as well as for her time serving with Paul. Now, she stood before the Roman church, trusting that they could all do the Lord's work together.

Paul's letter strengthened Phoebe's confidence. He commended her, which gave her credibility among the brothers and sisters she had just met. He had asked the people to give her any help she needed and told them that she had frequently been a benefactor to many, including himself. She was glad that her resources could be used by God, but this new season of ministry would require her to rely on the support of others.

The letter continued, greeting many more people in the room. It was clear that Paul had great fondness for these believers, even from a distance. Phoebe knew that the Holy Spirit was here in Rome just as it was back home. She was ready to walk alongside this church, to see what God had planned for their community, and to offer her leadership through sincere service.

JUNIA

Junia listened intently to the reading of Paul's letter. They hoped to see him here in Rome soon; but until then, his support strengthened their church. After they read his many thoughts and teachings, the letter concluded with greetings to various members of their group. Junia smiled at Priscilla as she was mentioned along with her husband, Aquila. She was also eager to speak with Phoebe, the deacon whom Paul had urged the Roman church to welcome and support.

When her own husband's name was read, Junia paid close attention and treasured every word. It had been a while since they had been with Paul, and his thoughtful remembrance filled her with gladness. He had written, "I send my greetings to Andronicus and Junia. They are also Jews, and have suffered with me in jail." Junia instantly thought of their nights on the cold stone floor, mouths dry with thirst and skin raw from rough chains. It had been one of the most difficult experiences of her life, but she would do it again if it meant that more people would hear the gospel.

The letter continued: "They followed Jesus even before me, and, out of many apostles, they are outstanding." How had it been so long since they began following Christ? Difficulties made time feel slow, but the love of their church community lifted her soul. When the days were cheerful and good, they seemed to pass quickly. So much had happened since Jesus walked among them, and Junia's life had been transformed. Tasks that once seemed routine were nearly forgotten as her priorities shifted to establishing and growing churches. Her days used to feel uneventful and ordinary; but now, her heart was dedicated to edifying and helping people increase their understanding. The final words of Paul's letter were read, and they spoke to her heart. God's message was being made known, and to Him be glory forever through Jesus Christ. Amen.

●●●●●●●●●●●●●●●●●●●●●●●●●●●●●●

Glimpses of women who followed Christ are woven into many New Testament passages. They're often brief and easily neglected amidst all the miracles and inspired instruction. But each name represents a person precious to God and instrumental in the life of His Church. Paul mentions women in leadership, as co-laborers, or as fellow servants, giving us clues about their roles. His greetings held few descriptions, suggesting that their work was well-known and familiar to recipients of his letters. These women stood out in a culture that was dominated by men by utilizing their abilities and resources to further the kingdom of God.

Tradition and societal norms leave many people on the sidelines still today. Voices are minimized based on gender, ethnicity, identity, ability, or other factors so that the status quo can remain. Yet God doesn't operate by cultural standards. Often His plans prompt us to step outside of traditional roles and go beyond society's expectations. God's power is not even slightly limited by human habits or preferences. In fact, His might is more evident when we break through social constraints.

Following Christ sometimes sets us apart. Paul advised us not to be like the world but instead to be changed by God as He renews our minds, preceding this with guidance to offer ourselves as a living sacrifice to God."[99] This means we reject earthly sinfulness and embrace God's commands, allowing Him to make us more like Jesus. The systems of this world aren't always compatible with the ways of God. For example, ancient Persian custom dictated specific procedures for communicating with a king, and those rules also applied to the queen. Yet Queen Esther tested those limits in order to speak to her husband and persuade him to take action to save her people. Jesus was also frequently counter-cultural, such as when He instructed disciples to refrain from the socially assumed practice of seeking revenge on enemies but to love them instead. [100] Additionally, He shared meals with people that society looked down upon, leading His new friends to turn away from sin and follow Him.

In the modern age, we live daily by biblical standards that set us apart from cultural norms. When we extend compassion to those who are marginalized—like the poor, sick, foreigners, or prisoners—we include people in God's love that many forget or even scorn. Our neighbors might not understand why we set aside a day to rest and worship, choosing a church service as they enjoy Sunday morning brunch, day trips to the beach, or a baseball game. Following

---

99 Romans 12:1-2
100 Matthew 5:33-38

God's guidelines for wealth is baffling in a world that adores money. The tax collector Zacchaeus exemplified generosity that's counterintuitive to society's love of wealth and self-interest. He left behind a dishonest life of taking money, gave half of his possessions to the poor, and then paid people four times the amount he took from them. We're also called to enthusiastically share our wealth, despite general acceptance of accumulating riches.

The women of the early church show us that God does remarkable things with His methods. The limits of patriarchal cultures aren't barriers to His care for us. Lydia, Priscilla, Nympha, Phoebe, Junia, and so many others were called to be instruments of kingdom work, carrying the love of Jesus near and far. Through them, God's power overcame obstacles rooted in ancient gender restrictions. In fact, being female became an asset, as it brought attention to a message that was meant for all. They encouraged other women to follow Christ along with them, as living proof that "there is neither Jew nor Gentile, neither slave nor free, nor is there male and female, for you are all one in Christ Jesus."[101]

Though continuing to follow traditions may preserve many benefits, daring to do something new creates different possibilities, including improvements. The potential to experience God's blessing is beyond what we can imagine! We make ourselves available to be part of His great work when we're not held back by cultural rules. God does the unexpected when we disregard unnecessary expectations.

These women did more than boldly break away from expected gender roles. They joined the rest of the early church to utilize their resources and care for their neighbors. When we have more than enough to meet our needs, we have a great opportunity to give. Some of the women who followed Jesus during His ministry financially supported Him. This included Joanna, the wife of Chuza, who was the manager of Herod's household. Her husband's position provided funds that she chose to share instead of keeping them for her own family. Later, the church in Acts completely committed to a

---

101 Galatians 3:28

communal lifestyle, selling possessions and sharing anything they had until there was no more need among them.

Sometimes on the sidelines, we find ourselves with more than we can use. This doesn't always mean extravagant wealth. An extra sandwich, a couple of dollars, or clothes forgotten in our closets can also be used by God to meet our neighbor's needs. Financial assets are helpful, but just as Nympha, Priscilla, and Lydia opened their homes, we, too, can offer other physical resources. A place to stay, transportation, or a meal can be tremendous gifts. We also might have a listening ear, practical skills, or available time. These are only a few examples of intangible things we can give when we feel we do not have much to share.

Good stewardship happens on the sidelines with results that extend beyond the present moment. Second Corinthians 9:6 reminds us that when we only sow a little, we only reap a little. However, sowing generously will yield greater results. We should give willingly and cheerfully, trusting that God will abundantly meet our needs. What's more, our generosity can go farther when we partner with others who are serving the Lord. Blessings from God provide us with additional things to offer, and our giving does more than only meet needs—it also expresses thanksgiving. We inspire others to see and praise the goodness of the Lord as they see His grace in action. We demonstrate our love for God by loving others, which includes sharing our resources.

The church came together in ways other than meeting the needs of their neighbors, and the women were instrumental in establishing community among the believers. They helped coordinate details and brought local Christ-followers together. Then a larger body of believers grew out of those local groups. Although these churches were scattered across great distances, they were connected through Paul, Priscilla and Aquila, Apollos, Phoebe, and many others who traveled between them. When necessary, some of the churches sent financial help to congregations who were in need. They supported one another in prayer and shared Paul's letters that he had sent to each of them.

Uniting people can be facilitated by our place on the sidelines as we assist in building communities. We can extend our relationships by connecting people with one another and encouraging new friendships. We're already familiar with living in the body of Christ, but it often requires our unique talents and specific abilities to begin the process of bringing neighbors together. Communities rarely form spontaneously; it takes effort and organization, and people on the sidelines are in an excellent position to help this happen. We can model the elements necessary for a healthy community to grow, like peacemaking, selflessness, and compassion. It might be challenging to establish a communal mindset while others are focused on individual concerns, but our persistence inspires others to join us.

To help our communities grow, we "spur one another on toward love and good deeds," as the writer of Hebrews 10:24 directed. This writer also pointed out that, even if some people have difficulty committing, we shouldn't give up on meeting together. Our consistency is crucial so that the group doesn't dissolve, and we can encourage those who drifted away to return. In this way, our steady presence on the sidelines helps our community grow from a basic foundation. Jesus said that where two or three meet together in His name, He would be among them. Just as the Philippian church started with a small group of women meeting by a river, our small beginnings often lead to something much bigger.

It takes boldness and bravery to join others and persuade individuals to coalesce into a cohesive unit. Patience and determination are required to endure what might be a long process with many challenges. Ultimately, it is God Who holds us together; no human being can maintain an entire community. However, the Lord involves us in these plans, and we are a vital member of the body of Christ.

Once again, we see that what we initially labeled as a "sideline" period is really a specially designed place where God includes us in His work. Everything that we've been given has the potential to become a blessing to someone else, as we encourage our neighbors and bring people together. When we realize that God has no limits, we see with more of His incredible perspective without being distracted by what the world says we can't do. We can welcome others like Lydia, share knowledge like Priscilla, lead like Nympha, unite people like Phoebe, and share Jesus like Junia. And then we will go on to fulfill God's purpose as ourselves.

Conclusion

When we started our journey, we acknowledged the seasons in our lives when we feel left behind, forgotten, or insignificant. However, without question, those seasons are extremely meaningful. God gives wonderful purpose to every person He created, and there are no exceptions. But a problem emerges when we compare ourselves to other people. We often think that their gifts are superior, their situations are better, and that they matter much more than we do. But that's not even slightly true.

God's definition of importance differs from ours. Humans tend to form hierarchies, but that's not the way His kingdom is designed. God sees every person as beloved, and He prepared good works for each of us. When we align our priorities with His, we value principles like loving our neighbors, seeking justice, and promoting peace. Comparing our distinct differences is a waste of time and prevents us from living fully.

But now that we've uncovered fundamental facts about the sidelines, we understand them in a new way. We learned that we aren't stranded in tough conditions. Seasons are, by definition, temporary. Though it often feels like time in the shadows stands still, we've come to realize that God will soon bring us into the light. He's with us even when we think we're alone.

Another fact: we don't find ourselves on the sidelines because we failed or earned a demotion. Life happens. Circumstances are often out of our control, and other people make choices that affect us. We will face consequences of our actions, but our purpose is not taken away from us when we make mistakes.

Though we can choose to walk away from God's plan, He forgives, redeems, and welcomes us when we return. The sidelines are not a punishment; so we can let go of guilt, shame, or condemnation when we're in difficult seasons.

Being out of the spotlight doesn't mean that we are in darkness. Beautiful things happen on the sidelines, and they are often wonderful in their own way. We can reframe our perspective and rejoice in the special gifts that can only be found there. It's often during these seasons that we become closer to God, trusting Him more as we walk with Him through our current challenges.

God's plans for us are starting to become a little clearer now. We're like pieces that complete a puzzle, placed exactly where we fit. Our lives are a canvas that displays God's glory, and the smallest matters are included in the masterpiece. Every quiet season has intention and is worth just as much as exciting occasions. As we grow to understand these aspects of God's purposes, encouragement replaces discouragement. This is yet another fact: we are growing more like Christ as we allow Him to direct us through trials. There's never a time when nothing is happening; though we may not see it, God is always doing something through His love for us.

We can be grateful for the people we've met in the pages of this book and for the things we learned from their stories. We might have missed them in our previous studies because our pastors or teachers don't often mention them. Or perhaps we simply didn't see them in familiar narratives because our eyes were on someone else, another person who seemed more important and in the thick of the action. We may have forgotten that the sideline-dwellers were humans like us, as complex and vulnerable as we are today, living through events that were no less real even though they occurred in the distant past. We previously allowed them to fade into the pages of our Bibles and become two-dimensional background characters.

But now we know better. We have walked with them and considered their lives. We imagined breathing in the clear air at Mount Carmel or pictured ourselves sitting by a river outside Philippi. We felt pressure to build a wall while fearing enemy attack. We experienced a mother's grief and celebrated bittersweet renewal. We discovered treasures between the lines of ancient text and met remarkable people who revealed lessons that apply to our own lives today.

Ham, Shem, and Japheth taught us that we have purpose even if we encounter opposition.

Lot's wife warned us of the consequences of rejecting God's plan and showed us that our heart's motivation determines our direction.

Benjamin encouraged us not to let others define us.

Jethro's hospitality opened the door to the gift of shared wisdom.

Caleb helped us understand that God truly sees us.

Eliab told us that God heals the sting of rejection, and that our purpose isn't always what we expect.

Gehazi highlighted our struggle between following God's heart and pursuing selfish ambitions.

Huldah inspired us to boldly speak the truth.

The sons of Hassenaah demonstrated the power of teamwork while trusting God.

Job's wife assured us that the Lord is with us through our pain and gives us hope for restoration.

The rooftop friend exemplified life-changing friendship and belief.

The temple merchant asked us how we respond when God corrects our mistakes.

Matthias gave us a look at the Lord's perfect timing.

Apollos humbly modeled the need to keep learning.

And the women of the early church urged us to love our neighbors in community.

The sidelines aren't what we thought they were. Perhaps they're not even sidelines at all. Life isn't really a show where we wait in the wings, nor is it a game that we watch from the bench. Instead, we've been invited to participate in the Creator's good plans, where every beloved child has a valued, essential place. We'll remember each of the people we met as we step back into our own stories and walk with God through whatever comes next. We're ready to love, encourage, and help wherever we're needed. We're equipped with courage, truth, and wisdom. We're exactly where we need to be to discover God's great purpose.

About the Author

When she isn't writing, Malinda Fugate serves as the children's education director at a church in Southern California. She earned a communications degree with a theater emphasis from Azusa Pacific University, then worked behind the scenes for Christian radio stations in Los Angeles.

Her writing includes *The Other Three Sixteens*, published by Ambassador International in May 2020, and the activity-filled devotional, *Bible Time for Active Kids*. Additionally, she has been a commercial copywriter and written various faith-based stage plays. She also co-produced "A Single Girls Guide To," a lifestyle blog and web series.

Malinda lives by the beach with her pup, Yoshi, where she often creates art, reads, or explores the many adventures to be found in her neighborhood and beyond.

CONTACT INFORMATION
Malindafugate.com
Facebook: @malthewriter
Twitter: @malthestar
Instagram: @malthewriter
malindafugate.substack.com

Ambassador International's mission is to magnify the Lord Jesus Christ and promote His Gospel through the written word.

We believe through the publication of Christian literature, Jesus Christ and His Word will be exalted, believers will be strengthened in their walk with Him, and the lost will be directed to Jesus Christ as the only way of salvation.

For more information about
AMBASSADOR INTERNATIONAL
please visit:

www.ambassador-international.com
@AmbassadorIntl
www.facebook.com/AmbassadorIntl

Thank you for reading this book!

You make it possible for us to fulfill our mission, and we are grateful for your partnership.

To help further our mission, please consider leaving us a review on your social media, favorite retailer's website, Goodreads or Bookbub, or our website, and check out some of the books on the following page!

THE JAW-DROPPING BEAUTY OF JESUS

JOSHUA WEST AND GARY WILKERSON
FOREWORD BY JIM CYMBALA

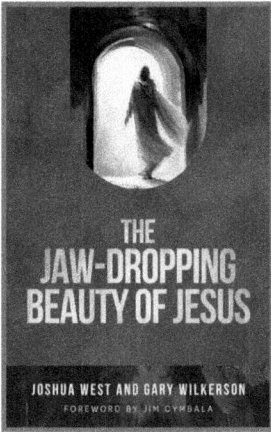

Most of us know Who Jesus is and would admit He was a good and kind Teacher while here on earth. But He is so much more than just a good and kind Teacher—He is our Savior and God and worthy of all our worship. Through an in-depth study into the book of Hebrews, Joshua West and Gary Wilkerson take apart each verse, drawing the reader to a closer look at the Man Who lived here on earth for a short time and then became our Sacrifice to save us from our sins and live with us eternally in Heaven with Him. If you are searching for something more from God, dive into this study and drink in the jaw-dropping beauty of our Jesus.

When our passions overtake us—as they often will—compulsive and addictive behaviors can set in. In *Misguided Passions and the Lord's Prayer*, Curt Richards examines the Lord's Prayer line by line and draws out comforting and reassuring insights that can be applied to the daily lives of anyone, especially those struggling with misguided passions. Richards shines a light on the beautiful universal truths found in the Lord's Prayer.

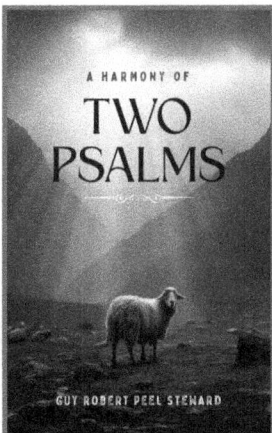

MISGUIDED PASSIONS &
the *Lord's Prayer*

CURT RICHARDS

A HARMONY OF TWO PSALMS

GUY ROBERT PEEL STEWARD

In a world that is full of chaos and change, many people turn to the Psalms to find comfort in times of stress. In *A Harmony of Two Psalms*, Guy Robert Peel Steward takes a closer look at two of those psalms—Psalm 2 and 91—and analyzes their key truths, hoping to shine some light for the reader on what the words truly mean and how they can find comfort in the God Who sees the chaos and offers rest in the storm. Be challenged in your knowledge of God's Word and learn more about some of the verses that can soothe our weary souls.